sweet bakes

essential recipes

Publisher's Note:
Raw or semi-cooked eggs should not be consumed by babies, toddlers,
pregnant women, the elderly or those suffering from recurring illness.

This is a **FLAME TREE** book
First published in 2012

Publisher and Creative Director: Nick Wells
Project Editor: Catherine Taylor
Art Director: Mike Spender
Layout Design: Jane Ashley
Operations Manager: Chris Herbert
Proofreader: Dawn Laker
Photographers: Paul Forrester, Colin Bowling and Stephen Brayne
Home Economists & Stylists: Gina Steer, Ann Nicol, Jaqueline Bellefontaine,
Mandy Phipps, Vicki Smallwood and Penny Stephens

Special thanks to Laura Bulbeck.

12 14 16 15 13

1 3 5 7 9 10 8 6 4 2

This edition first published 2012 by
FLAME TREE PUBLISHING
Crabtree Hall, Crabtree Lane
Fulham, London SW6 6TY
United Kingdom

www.flametreepublishing.com

Flame Tree is part of The Foundry Creative Media Co. Ltd
© 2012 The Foundry Creative Media Co. Ltd

ISBN 978-0-85775-386-1

A CIP Record for this book is available from the British Library upon request

Printed in China

sweet bakes

essential recipes

General Editor: Gina Steer

**FLAME TREE
PUBLISHING**

Contents

Puddings & Decadent Desserts

Equipment

Cooking equipment not only assists, but can make all the difference between success and failure. A few well-picked, high-quality pieces of equipment will be frequently used and will therefore be a much wiser buy than cheaper gadgets.

Baking Equipment

Follow the manufacturer's instructions when first using a tin and ensure that it is thoroughly washed and dried after use. There are many cake and loaf tins available – such as sandwich cake tins and deep cake tins, of many sizes, in round, square and oblong shapes – but for the recipes in this book there are other items that will be of more use, though deep 20.5 cm/8 inch cake tins are useful for cake puddings.

Good baking sheets are a must. Dishes that are too hot to handle such as apple pies should be placed directly onto a baking tray. Meringues and biscuits are also cooked on a baking tray. Do not confuse these with Swiss roll tins which have sides all around: a sheet only has one raised side.

Square or oblong shallow baking tins are also very useful for making tray bakes, brownies, flapjacks and shortbread. Patty tins are ideal for making small buns, jam tarts or mince pies, while individual Yorkshire pudding tins and muffin tins are also useful. They are available in a variety of sizes. There are plenty of other tins to choose from, from themed and shaped, to spring-form tins where the sides release after cooking, allowing the cake to be removed easily. Three to four different sizes of mixing bowls are also very useful.

Another piece of equipment worth having is a wire cooling rack. It is essential when baking to allow biscuits and cakes to cool after being removed from their tins.

A selection of ovenproof ceramic dishes are useful for making puddings such as bread pudding. Ramekin dishes and small pudding basins can be used for a variety of different recipes, as can small tartlet tins and dariole moulds.

Perhaps the rolling pin is one of the most important baking implements. Ideally it should be long and thin, heavy enough to roll the pastry out easily but not too heavy that it is uncomfortable to use. Pastry needs to be rolled out on a flat surface, and although a lightly floured flat surface will do, a marble slab will keep the pastry cool and ensure that the fats do not melt while being rolled. This helps to keep the pastry light, crisp and flaky rather than heavy and stodgy.

Other useful basic pastry implements are tools such as a pastry brush (which can be used to wet pastry or brush on a glaze), a pastry wheel for cutting and a sieve to remove impurities and also to sift air into the flour, encouraging the pastry or mixture to be lighter in texture.

Basic mixing cutlery is also essential, such as a wooden spoon (for mixing and creaming), a spatula (for transferring the mixture from the mixing bowl to the baking tins and spreading the mixture once it is in the tins) and a palette knife (to ease cakes and breads out of their tins before placing them on the wire racks to cool). Measuring spoons and cups are essential for accurate measuring of both dry and wet ingredients.

Baking Papers

Greaseproof paper has been around for many years. Unlike waxed paper and nonstick baking parchment, it does need oiling lightly. It has many uses including lining of baking sheets, tray and tins. Waxed paper is also used, though is less widely available. It is made moisture-proof by the application of wax. When using, it is not necessary to use any oil. It can also be used to wrap cooked biscuits, as it will keep the moisture out so that they retain their crisp texture.

You are more likely to find nonstick baking paper or baking parchment, which is now used extensively in baking and often replaces greaseproof paper. There is often no need to oil when lining tins; however, a little oil is useful, as it helps to keep the paper together and in one place.

Silicone-treated baking paper is specially made for baking and can be used time and time again, as it is washable. It comes in a roll or ready-cut; simply place a sheet on the baking sheet. There are also ready-cut pieces that fit the base and sides of cake tins. It can also be used to wrap food that will be cooked in the oven or the microwave, as well as for storing food in the refrigerator and freezer. It is made from unbleached parchment paper.

Electrical Equipment

Nowadays help from time-saving gadgets and electrical equipment make baking far easier and quicker. Equipment can be used for creaming, mixing, beating, whisking, kneading, grating and chopping. There is a wide choice available, from the most basic to the very sophisticated.

Food Processors

When choosing a machine, you must first decide what you need it to do. If you are a novice, it may be a waste to start with a machine that offers a wide range of implements and functions. This can be off-putting and result in not using the machine to its full capabilities.

In general, while styling and product design play a role in the price, the more you pay, the larger the machine will be, with a bigger bowl capacity and many more gadgets attached. However, just what basic features should you ensure your machine has before buying it? When buying a food processor look for measurements on the side of the processor bowl and machines with a removable feed tube which allows food or liquid to be added while the motor is still running. Look out for machines that have the facility to increase the capacity of the bowl (ideal when making soup) and have a pulse button for controlled chopping.

It is also worth thinking about machines that offer optional extras that can be bought as your requirements change. For instance, mini chopping bowls are available for those wanting to chop small quantities of food. If time is an issue, dishwasher-friendly attachments may be vital.

Blenders

Blenders often come as attachments to food processors and are generally used for liquidising and puréeing. There are two main types. The first is known as a goblet blender. The blades are at the bottom of the goblet with measurements up the sides. The second is portable. It is handheld and should be placed in a bowl to blend.

Food Mixers

These are ideally suited to mixing cakes and puddings and kneading dough, and are either table-top or handheld. The table-top mixers are freestanding and are capable of dealing with fairly large quantities. They are robust and capable of easily dealing with kneading and heavy cake mixing as well as whipping cream, whisking egg whites or making one-stage cakes. Handheld mixers are smaller and often come with their own bowl and stand from which they can be lifted off and used as handheld devices. They have a motorised head with detachable whisks. These mixers are particularly versatile as any suitable mixing bowl can be used.

Basic Techniques

There is no mystery to successful baking; it really is easy providing you follow a few simple rules. First, read the recipe right through before commencing. Until you are confident with a recipe do not try any short cuts, or you may find that you have left out a vital step.

Pastry Making

Pastry needs to be kept as cool as possible throughout. Cool hands help. Use cold or iced water, but not too much as pastry does not need to be wet. Make sure that your fat is not runny or melted but firm (this is why block fat is the best). Avoid using too much flour when rolling as this alters the proportions, and also avoid handling the dough too much. Roll in one direction as this ensures that the pastry does not shrink. Allow pastry to rest after rolling, preferably in the refrigerator. If your pastry is still not as good as you would like it to be, then make it in a processor instead.

Lining a Flan Case

It is important to choose the right tin to bake with. You will often find that a loose-bottomed metal flan case is the best option as it conducts heat more efficiently and evenly than a ceramic dish. It also has the added advantage of a removable base, which makes the transfer of the final flan or tart a much simpler process.

Roll the pastry out on a lightly floured surface ensuring that it is a few inches larger than the flan case. Wrap the pastry around the rolling pin, lift and place in the tin. Carefully ease the pastry into the base and sides of the tin. Allow to rest for a few minutes then trim the edge with a sharp knife or by rolling a rolling pin across the top of the tin.

Baking Blind

The term baking blind means that the pastry case needs to be cooked without the filling, resulting in a crisp pastry shell that is either partially or fully cooked depending on whether

the filling needs any cooking. Pastry shells can be prepared ahead of time, as they last for several days if stored correctly in an airtight container or longer if frozen.

To bake blind, line the tin or dish with the prepared pastry and allow to rest in the refrigerator for 30 minutes. This will help to minimise shrinkage while it is being cooked. Then lightly prick the base all over with a fork (do not do this if the filling is runny). Brush with a little beaten egg if desired or simply line the case with a large square of greaseproof paper, big enough to cover both the base and sides. Fill with ceramic baking beans, dried beans or rice. Place on a baking sheet and bake in a preheated oven, generally at 200°C/400°F/Gas Mark 6, remembering that ovens can take at least 15 minutes to reach this temperature. Cook for 10–12 minutes, then remove from the oven and discard the paper and beans. Return to the oven and continue to cook for a further 5–10 minutes depending on whether the filling needs cooking.

Covering a Pie Dish

To cover a pie, roll out the pastry until it is about 2 inches larger than the circumference of the dish. Cut a 2.5 cm/1 inch strip from around the outside of the pastry and then moisten the edge of the pie dish you are using. Place the strip on the edge of the dish and brush with water or beaten egg. Generously fill the pie dish until the surface is slightly rounded. Using the rolling pin, lift the remaining pastry and cover the pie dish. Press together to seal. Using a sharp knife, trim off any excess pastry from around the edges. Try to avoid brushing the edges of the pastry, especially puff pastry, as this prevents the pastry rising evenly. Make a small hole in the centre of the pie to allow the steam to escape.

The edges of the pie can be forked by pressing the back of a fork around the edge of the pie, or instead crimp by pinching the edge crust with thumb and index finger. Further decorate by putting leaves and berries made out of leftover pastry on top of the pie, then brush the top with beaten egg.

Lining Tins

If a recipe states that the tin needs lining, do not be tempted to ignore this. Rich fruit cakes and other cakes that take a long time to cook benefit from the tin being lined so that the edges and base do not burn or dry out, but other puddings also require a certain amount of lining. Greaseproof paper or baking parchment is ideal for this. It is a good idea to have the paper at least double thickness, or preferably 3–4 thicknesses.

The best way to line a round or square tin is to lightly draw around the base and then cut just inside the markings so it sits easily inside the tin. Next, lightly oil the paper so it easily peels away from the cake. If the sides of the tin also need to be lined, then cut a strip of paper long enough for the tin. This can be measured by wrapping a piece of string around the rim of the tin. Once again, lightly oil the paper, push against the tin and oil once more, as this will hold the paper to the sides of the tin. Steamed puddings usually need only a disc of greaseproof paper at the bottom of the dish.

Hints for Successful Baking

Ensure that the ingredients are accurately measured, or your pastries, biscuits and puddings will not have the right texture or may or may not rise depending on what is required.

Ensure that the oven is preheated to the correct temperature – it can take 10 minutes to reach 180°C/350°F/Gas Mark 4. You may find that an oven thermometer is a good investment. Items are best if cooked in the centre of the oven. Do try to avoid the temptation to open the oven door at the beginning, as a draught can make certain things, such as cakey puddings, sink. If using a fan oven, refer to the manufacturer's instructions, as they normally cook 10–20° hotter than conventional ovens.

When you take your items out of the oven, unless the recipe states that they should be left in the tin until cold, leave for a few minutes and then loosen the edges and transfer onto a wire rack to cool. Bakes that are left in the tin for too long tend to sink or slightly overcook. When storing, make sure products are completely cold before placing it into an airtight tin or plastic container.

Culinary Terms Explained

At a glance, here are some more key terms you will come across when baking. Some we may have discussed already, some may be new to you.

Baking powder A raising agent which works by producing carbon dioxide as a consequence of a reaction caused by the acid and alkali ingredients which expand during the baking process and make the breads and cakes rise.

Bicarbonate of soda This alkali powder acts as a raising agent in baking when combined with an acid or acid liquid (cream of tartar, lemon juice, yogurt, buttermilk, cocoa or vinegar, for example).

Cream of tartar An acid raising agent (potassium hydrogen tartrate) often present in both self-raising flour and baking powder. Activates the alkali component of baking powder.

Cornflour Used to thicken consistency and can also be used in meringue-making to prevent the meringue becoming hard and brittle and to enhance its chewiness.

Curdling When the milk separates from a sauce through acidity or excessive heat. This can also happen to creamed cake mixtures that have separated due to the eggs being too cold or added too quickly.

Sifting The shaking of dry ingredients (primarily flour) through a metal or nylon sieve to remove lumps and impurities, and to add air.

Binding Adding liquid or egg to bring a dry mixture together. Normally, this entails using a fork, spoon or your fingertips.

Creaming The method by which fat and sugar are beaten together until lighter in colour and fluffy. By creaming the fat in cake mixtures, air is incorporated into the fairly high fat content. It thus lightens the texture of cakes and puddings.

Folding A method of combining creamed fat and sugar with flour in cake and pudding mixes, usually by carefully mixing with a large metal spoon, either by cutting and folding or by doing a figure-of-eight, in order to maintain a light texture.

Rubbing in The method of combining fat with flour by rubbing them together using your hands. For crumble toppings, shortcrust pastry, biscuits and scones.

Beating The method by which air is introduced into a mixture using a fork, wooden spoon, whisk or electric mixer. Beating is also used as a method of softening ingredients.

Whipping/whisking The term given to incorporating air rapidly into a mixture (either through using a manual whisk or an electric whisk).

Dropping consistency The consistency that a cake or pudding mixture reaches before being cooked. It tends to be fairly soft (but not runny) and should drop off a spoon in around 5 seconds when tapped lightly on the side of a bowl.

Rice paper This edible paper is made from the pith of a Chinese tree and can be used as a base on which to bake delicate or sticky cakes and biscuits such as almond macaroons.

Choux A type of pastry whose uncooked dough is rather like a glossy batter, which is piped into small balls onto a baking sheet and baked until light and airy. They can then be filled with cream or savoury fillings.

Filo A type of pastry that is wafer-thin. Three to four sheets are usually used at a time, buttered, then layered.

Puff pastry Probably the richest of pastries, as it is enriched with a high proportion of butter, which makes a pastry with light flaky layers. When making from the beginning, it requires the lightest of handling.

Brioche A sweet spongy traditional bread eaten in France for breakfast, often served warm. Brioche is enriched with eggs and butter and has a rich but soft texture, made from a very light yeast dough, and is baked in the shape of a small cottage loaf. A delicious substitute for bread in bread and butter pudding.

Caramel Obtained by heating sugar on a very low heat until it turns liquid and deep brown in colour. This is used in dishes such as crème caramel, which is, in turn, baked in a bain-marie.

Bain-marie A French term meaning water bath. A shallow tin, often a roasting tin, is half-filled with water; smaller dishes of food are then placed in it, allowing them to cook at lower temperatures without overheating. This method is often used to cook custards and other egg dishes or to keep some dishes warm.

Ramekin An ovenproof earthenware dish which provides an individual serving. 'Cocotte' is another name for a ramekin.

Dariole A small narrow mould with sloping sides used for making Madeleines. Darioles can also be used for individual steamed or baked puddings and jellies.

Dusting To sprinkle lightly, often with flour, sugar or icing sugar. Similar to 'dredging', which may be considered to be heavier.

Glacé A French term meaning glossy or iced. Glacé icing is a quick icing often used to decorate cakes and biscuits. It is made using icing sugar and warm water.

Piping A way in which cakes and desserts are decorated, or the method by which choux pastry is placed onto a baking sheet. This is achieved by putting cream, icing or mixture in a nylon bag (with a nozzle attached), or an improvised piping bag made from a cone of greaseproof paper, and then slowly forcing through the nozzle and piping it onto the cake or baking sheet.

Zest This can refer to the outer coloured part of an orange, lemon or lime peel, or the very thin pieces of that peel. The zest contains the fruit oil, which is responsible for the citrus flavour. Normally, a zester is used to create the strips, as it removes the zest without any of the bitter white pith. Zest can also be grated on a grater into very small pieces, again taking care to only remove the very outer layer.

Pies & Pastry

There is a whole world of pastry and pies out there – from delicate tartlets to hearty fruit pies, from sculpted filo creations to fluffy choux pastry delights. In this tempting section, take your pick from a refreshing Goats' Cheese & Lemon Tart or a luxuriant Chocolate Mallow Pie, try your hand at a classic Lemon Meringue Pie or a homely Rhubarb & Raspberry Cobbler – there's something for everyone!

Orange Curd & Plum Pie

1 Preheat the oven to 200°C/400°F/Gas Mark 6. Lightly oil a 20.5 cm/8 inch round cake tin. Cook the plums with 2 tablespoons of the light brown sugar for 8–10 minutes to soften them, remove from the heat and reserve.

2 Mix together the zest, butter and oil. Lay a sheet of pastry in the prepared cake tin and brush with the lemon zest mixture.

3 Cut the sheets of filo pastry in half and then place one half sheet in the cake tin and brush again.

4 Top with the remaining halved sheets of pastry, brushing each time with the lemon zest mixture. Fold each sheet in half lengthways to line the sides of the tin to make a filo case.

5 Mix the orange curd and sultanas into the plums and spoon into the pastry case.

6 Draw the pastry edges up over the filling to enclose. Brush the remaining sheets of filo pastry with the lemon zest mixture and cut into thick strips.

7 Scrunch each strip of pastry and arrange on top of the pie. Bake in the preheated oven for 25 minutes until golden. Sprinkle with icing sugar and serve with the Greek yogurt.

Ingredients   SERVES 4

700 g/1½ lb plums, stoned
    and quartered
2 tbsp light brown sugar
grated zest of ½ lemon
25 g/1 oz butter, melted
1 tbsp olive oil
6 sheets filo pastry
½ x 411 g jar luxury orange curd
50 g/2 oz sultanas
icing sugar, to decorate
half–fat thick set Greek yogurt,
    to serve

Helpful Hint
Filo pastry dries out very quickly.
Keep wrapped when not using.

Raspberry & Almond Tart

1 Preheat the oven to 200°C/400°F/Gas Mark 6, 15 minutes before cooking. Blend the flour, salt and butter in a food processor until the mixture resembles breadcrumbs. Add the sugar and lemon zest and blend again for 1 minute. Mix the egg yolk with 2 tablespoons of cold water and add to the mixture. Blend until the mixture starts to come together, adding a little more water if necessary, then tip out onto a lightly floured surface. Knead until smooth, wrap in clingfilm and chill in the refrigerator for 30 minutes.

2 Roll the dough out thinly on a lightly floured surface and use to line a 23 cm/9 inch fluted tart tin. Chill in the refrigerator for 10 minutes. Line the pastry case with greaseproof paper and baking beans. Bake for 10 minutes, then remove the paper and beans and return to the oven for a further 10–12 minutes until cooked. Allow to cool slightly, then reduce the oven temperature to 190°C/375°F/Gas Mark 5.

3 Blend together the butter, sugar, ground almonds and eggs until smooth. Spread the raspberries over the base of the pastry, then cover with the almond mixture. Bake for 15 minutes. Remove from the oven and sprinkle with the slivered or flaked almonds and dust generously with icing sugar. Bake for a further 15–20 minutes until firm and golden brown. Leave to cool, then serve.

Ingredients   SERVES 6–8

For the pastry:
225 g/8 oz plain flour
pinch salt
125 g/4 oz butter, cut into pieces
50 g/2 oz caster sugar
grated zest of $\frac{1}{2}$ lemon
1 medium egg yolk

For the filling:
75 g/3 oz butter
75 g/3 oz caster sugar
75 g/3 oz ground almonds
2 medium eggs
225 g/8 oz raspberries, thawed if frozen
2 tbsp slivered or flaked almonds
icing sugar, for dusting

Tasty Tip
Omit the raspberries in the above tart. Spread the almond mixture over the base of the pastry case and top with poached or drained tinned pear halves. Scatter over flaked almonds and bake as above.

1

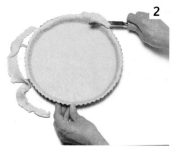
2

3

Goats' Cheese & Lemon Tart

1. Preheat the oven to 200°C/400°F/Gas Mark 6, 15 minutes before cooking. Rub the butter into the plain flour and salt until the mixture resembles breadcrumbs, then stir in the sugar. Beat the egg yolk with 2 tablespoons of cold water and add to the mixture. Mix together until a dough is formed, then turn the dough out onto a lightly floured surface and knead until smooth. Chill in the refrigerator for 30 minutes.

2. Roll the dough out thinly on a lightly floured surface and use to line a 4 cm/1½ inch deep 23 cm/9 inch fluted flan tin. Chill in the refrigerator for 10 minutes. Line the pastry case with greaseproof paper and baking beans or foil and bake blind in the preheated oven for 10 minutes. Remove the paper and beans or foil. Return to the oven for a further 12–15 minutes until cooked. Leave to cool slightly, then reduce the oven temperature to 150°C/300°F/Gas Mark 2.

3. Beat the goats' cheese until smooth. Whisk in the eggs, sugar, lemon zest and juice. Add the cream and mix well.

4. Carefully pour the cheese mixture into the pastry case and return to the oven. Bake in the oven for 35–40 minutes until just set. If it begins to brown or swell, open the oven door for 2 minutes, then reduce the temperature to 120°C/250°F/Gas Mark ½ and leave the tart to cool in the oven. Chill in the refrigerator until cold. Decorate and serve with fresh raspberries.

Ingredients   SERVES 8–10

For the pastry:
125 g/4 oz butter, cut into small
   pieces
225 g/8 oz plain flour
pinch salt
50 g/2 oz caster sugar
1 medium egg yolk

For the filling:
350 g/12 oz mild fresh goats'
   cheese, e.g. Chavroux
3 medium eggs, beaten
150 g/5 oz caster sugar
grated zest and juice of 3 lemons
450 ml/³/₄ pint double cream
fresh raspberries, to decorate
   and serve

Tasty Tip
The goat's cheese adds a certain unusual piquancy to this tart. Substitute full-fat soft cheese or ricotta, if preferred.

1

3

4

Passion Fruit & Pomegranate Citrus Tart

1 Preheat the oven to 200°C/400°F/Gas Mark 6. Sift the flour and salt into a large bowl and rub in the butter until the mixture resembles fine breadcrumbs. Stir in the sugar. Whisk the egg yolk and add to the dry ingredients. Mix well to form a smooth, pliable dough. Knead gently on a lightly floured surface until smooth. Wrap the pastry and leave to rest in the refrigerator for 30 minutes.

2 Roll out the pastry on a lightly floured surface and use to line a 25.5 cm/10 inch loose-based flan tin. Line the pastry case with greaseproof paper and baking beans. Brush the edges of the pastry with the egg white and bake blind in the preheated oven for 15 minutes. Remove the paper and beans and bake for 5 minutes. Remove and reduce the temperature to 180°C/350°F/Gas Mark 4.

3 Halve the passion fruit and spoon the flesh into a bowl. Whisk the sugar and eggs together in a bowl. When mixed thoroughly, stir in the double cream with the passion fruit juice and flesh and the lime juice.

4 Pour the mixture into the pastry case and bake for 30–40 minutes until the filling is just set. Remove and cool slightly, then chill in the refrigerator for 1 hour. Cut the pomegranate in half and scoop the seeds into a sieve. Spoon the drained seeds over the top and just before serving dust with icing sugar.

Ingredients SERVES 4

For the pastry:
175 g/6 oz plain flour
pinch salt
125 g/4 oz butter
4 tsp caster sugar
1 small egg, separated

For the filling:
2 passion fruit
175 g/6 oz caster sugar
4 large eggs
175 ml/6 fl oz double cream
3 tbsp lime juice
1 pomegranate
icing sugar, for dusting

Helpful Hint

Pomegranates have leathery skin and may be a dark yellow to a crimson colour. They have a distinctive slightly acidic flavour.

1

1

3

Luxury Mince Pies

1 Sift the flour and ground almonds into a bowl or a food processor and add the butter. Rub in or process until the mixture resembles fine crumbs. Sift in the icing sugar and stir in the lemon zest. Whisk the egg yolk and milk together in a separate bowl and stir into the mixture until a soft dough forms. Wrap the pastry in clingfilm and chill for 30 minutes.

2 Preheat the oven to 200°C/400°F/Gas Mark 6. Grease two 12-hole patty tins. Roll out the pastry on a lightly floured surface to 3 mm/⅛ inch thickness. Cut out 20 rounds using a 7.5 cm/3 inch fluted round pastry cutter. Re-roll the trimmings into thin strips.

3 Mix the filling ingredients together in a bowl. Place 1 tablespoon of the filling in each pastry case, then dampen the edges of each case with a little water. Put four strips of pastry over the top of each case to form a lattice.

4 Bake for 10–15 minutes until the pastry is crisp. Dust with icing sugar and serve hot or cold.

Ingredients MAKES 20

For the pastry:
275 g/10 oz plain flour
25 g/1 oz ground almonds
175 g/6 oz butter, diced
75 g/3 oz icing sugar
zest of 1 lemon, finely grated
1 egg yolk
3 tbsp milk

For the filling:
225 g/8 oz mincemeat
1 tbsp dark rum or orange juice
zest of 1 orange, finely grated
75 g/3 oz dried cranberries
icing sugar, for dusting

Mocha Pie

1 Place the prepared pastry case on a large serving plate and reserve. Melt the chocolate in a heatproof bowl set over a saucepan of simmering water. Ensure the water is not touching the base of the bowl. Remove from the heat, stir until smooth and leave to cool.

2 Cream the butter, soft brown sugar and vanilla extract until light and fluffy, then beat in the cooled chocolate. Add the strong black coffee, pour into the pastry case and chill in the refrigerator for about 30 minutes.

3 For the topping, whisk the cream until beginning to thicken, then whisk in the sugar and vanilla extract. Continue to whisk until the cream is softly peaking. Spoon just under half of the cream into a separate bowl and fold in the dissolved coffee.

4 Spread the remaining cream over the filling in the pastry case. Spoon the coffee-flavoured whipped cream evenly over the top, then swirl it decoratively with a palate knife. Sprinkle with grated chocolate and chill in the refrigerator until ready to serve.

Ingredients   SERVES 4–6

1 x 23 cm/9 inch ready-made sweet
  pastry case

For the filling:
125 g/4 oz dark chocolate, broken
  into pieces
175 g/6 oz unsalted butter
225 g/8 oz soft brown sugar
1 tsp vanilla extract
3 tbsp strong black coffee

For the topping:
600 ml/1 pint double cream
50 g/2 oz icing sugar
2 tsp vanilla extract
1 tsp instant coffee dissolved in
  1 tsp boiling water and cooled
grated plain and white chocolate,
  to decorate

Helpful Hint
Using a ready-made pastry case makes this a quickly made store-cupboard pie that looks very impressive.

White Chocolate Eclairs

1 Preheat the oven to 190°C/375°F/Gas Mark 5, 10 minutes before baking. Lightly oil a baking sheet. Place the butter and 150 ml/¹/₄ pint water in a saucepan and heat until the butter has melted, then bring to the boil. Remove from the heat and immediately add the flour all at once, beating with a wooden spoon until the mixture forms a ball. Leave to cool for 3 minutes. Add the eggs a little at a time, beating well after each addition until the paste is smooth, shiny and of a piping consistency.

2 Spoon the mixture into a piping bag fitted with a plain nozzle. Sprinkle the oiled baking sheet with water. Pipe the mixture onto the baking sheet in 7.5 cm/3 inch lengths, using a knife to cut each pastry length neatly. Bake in the preheated oven for 18–20 minutes until well risen and golden. Make a slit along the side of each eclair to let the steam escape. Return the eclairs to the oven for a further 2 minutes to dry out. Transfer to a wire rack and leave to cool.

3 Halve the passion fruit and, using a small spoon, scoop the pulp of 4 of the fruits into a bowl. Add the cream, kirsch and icing sugar and whip until the cream holds its shape. Carefully spoon or pipe into the eclairs. Melt the chocolate in a small heatproof bowl set over a saucepan of simmering water and stir until smooth. Leave to cool slightly, then spread over the tops of the eclairs. Scoop the pulp out of the remaining fruits. Sieve. Drizzle the juice around the eclairs and serve.

Ingredients SERVES 4–6

50 g/2 oz unsalted butter
60 g/2¹/₂ oz plain flour, sifted
2 medium eggs, lightly beaten
6 ripe passion fruit
300 ml/¹/₂ pint double cream
3 tbsp kirsch
1 tbsp icing sugar
125 g/4 oz white chocolate, broken
    into pieces

Helpful Hint

Passion fruit are readily available in supermarkets. They are small round purplish fruits that should have quite wrinkled skins. Smooth passion fruit are not ripe and will have little juice or flavour.

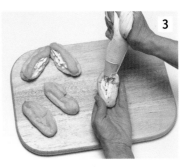

Chocolate Mallow Pie

1 This recipe actually isn't baked, but it seemed to good not to include! Lightly oil an 18 cm/7 inch flan tin. Place the biscuits in a polythene bag and finely crush with a rolling pin. Alternatively, place in a food processor and blend until fine crumbs are formed.

2 Melt the butter in a medium-sized saucepan, add the crushed biscuits and mix together. Press into the base of the prepared tin and leave to cool in the refrigerator.

3 Melt 125 g/4 oz of the chocolate with the marshmallows and 2 tablespoons of water in a saucepan over a gentle heat, stirring constantly. Leave to cool slightly, then stir in the egg yolk, beat well, then leave in the refrigerator until cool.

4 Whisk the egg white until stiff and standing in peaks, then fold into the chocolate mixture.

5 Lightly whip the cream and fold three-quarters of the cream into the chocolate mixture. Reserve the remainder. Spoon the chocolate cream into the flan tin and chill in the refrigerator until set.

6 When ready to serve, spoon the remaining cream over the chocolate pie, swirling in a decorative pattern. Grate the remaining dark chocolate and sprinkle over the cream, then serve.

Ingredients   SERVES 6

200 g/7 oz digestive biscuits
75 g/3 oz butter, melted
175 g/6 oz dark chocolate
20 marshmallows
1 medium egg, separated
300 ml/$^1/_2$ pint double cream

Tasty Tip

Replace the digestive biscuits with an equal weight of chocolate-covered digestive biscuits to make a quick change to this recipe.

Puff Pastry Jalousie

1. Preheat the oven to 200°C/400°F/Gas Mark 6 and grease a large baking sheet. Grate the apples coarsely, then mix together with the mincemeat, orange zest and the marmalade, then reserve.

2. Place the pastry on a lightly floured surface and cut it in half. Roll each piece into an 18 x 25 cm/7 x 10 inch rectangle. Place one of the rectangles on the baking sheet.

3. Spoon the filling down the middle, leaving a 2.5 cm/1 inch edge all round. Brush the pastry edges with the beaten egg. Score thin lines across the middle of the remaining pastry rectangle right through the pastry, leaving a plain narrow 2.5 cm/1 inch rim all round. Lift the scored pastry on top of the filling and press the edges together to seal.

4. Brush the pastry with the beaten egg and bake for about 30 minutes until golden and crisp. Sprinkle generously with caster sugar and return to the oven for 5 minutes. Serve hot with custard or double cream.

Ingredients   SERVES 6–8

2 large dessert apples, peeled
  and cored
4 tbsp mincemeat
zest of 1 orange, finely grated
1 tbsp orange marmalade
350 g/12 oz puff pastry
1 medium egg, beaten
caster sugar, for sprinkling
custard or double cream,
  to serve

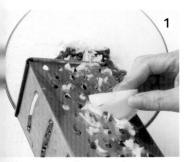

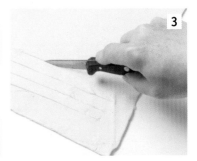

Chocolate, Orange & Pine Nut Tart

1 Preheat the oven to 200°C/400°F/Gas Mark 6, 15 minutes before baking. Place the flour, salt and sugar in a food processor with the butter and blend briefly. Add the egg yolks, 2 tablespoons of iced water and the vanilla extract and blend until a soft dough is formed. Remove and knead until smooth, wrap in clingfilm and chill in the refrigerator for 1 hour.

2 Lightly oil a 23 cm/9 inch loose-based flan tin. Roll the dough out on a lightly floured surface to a 28 cm/11 inch round and use to line the tin. Press into the sides of the flan tin, crimp the edges, prick the base with a fork and chill in the refrigerator for 1 hour. Bake blind in the preheated oven for 10 minutes. Remove and place on a baking sheet. Reduce the oven temperature to 190°C/375°F/Gas Mark 5.

3 To make the filling, sprinkle the chocolate and the pine nuts evenly over the base of the pastry case. Beat the eggs, orange zest, Cointreau and cream in a bowl until well blended, then pour over the chocolate and pine nuts.

4 Bake in the oven for 30 minutes, or until the pastry is golden and the custard mixture is just set. Transfer to a wire rack to cool slightly. Heat the marmalade with 1 tablespoon of water and brush over the tart. Serve warm or at room temperature.

Ingredients   SERVES 8–10

For the sweet shortcrust pastry:
150 g/5 oz plain flour
1/2 tsp salt
3–4 tbsp icing sugar
125 g/4 oz unsalted butter, diced
2 medium egg yolks, beaten
1/2 tsp vanilla extract

For the filling:
125 g/4 oz dark chocolate, chopped
65 g/21/2 oz pine nuts, lightly toasted
2 large eggs
grated zest of 1 orange
1 tbsp Cointreau
225 ml/8 fl oz whipping cream
2 tbsp orange marmalade

Food Fact
Cointreau is an orange-flavoured liqueur and is used in many recipes. You could substitute Grand Marnier or any other orange liqueur, if you prefer.

Chocolate Pecan Pie

1 Preheat the oven to 180°C/350°F/Gas Mark 4, 10 minutes before baking. Roll the prepared pastry out on a lightly floured surface and use to line a 25.5 cm/10 inch pie plate. Roll the trimmings out and use to make a decorative edge around the pie, then chill in the refrigerator for 1 hour.

2 Reserve about 60 perfect pecan halves, or enough to cover the top of the pie, then coarsely chop the remainder and reserve. Melt the chocolate and butter in a small saucepan over a low heat or in the microwave and reserve.

3 Beat the eggs and brush the base and sides of the pastry with a little of the beaten egg. Beat the sugar, golden syrup and vanilla extract into the beaten eggs. Add the pecans, then beat in the chocolate mixture.

4 Pour the filling into the pastry case and arrange the reserved pecan halves in concentric circles over the top. Bake in the preheated oven for 45–55 minutes until the filling is well risen and just set. If the pastry edge begins to brown too quickly, cover with strips of foil. Remove from the oven and serve with ice cream.

Ingredients SERVES 8–10

225 g/8 oz prepared shortcrust pastry (see page 32)
200 g/7 oz pecan halves
125 g/4 oz dark chocolate, chopped
25 g/1 oz butter, diced
3 medium eggs
125 g/4 oz light brown sugar
175 ml/6 fl oz golden syrup
2 tsp vanilla extract
vanilla ice cream, to serve

Helpful Hint

The pastry case in this recipe is not baked blind, but the pie does not become soggy because of the long cooking time, which allows the pastry to become crisp.

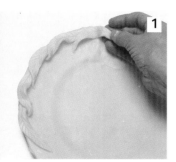

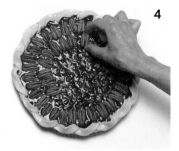

Pear & Chocolate Custard Tart

1 Preheat the oven to 190°C/375°F/Gas Mark 5, 10 minutes before baking. To make the pastry, put the butter, sugar and vanilla extract into a food processor and blend until creamy. Add the flour and cocoa and process until a soft dough forms. Remove, wrap in clingfilm and chill in the refrigerator for at least 1 hour. Roll out the dough between two sheets of clingfilm to a 28 cm/11 inch round. Peel off the top sheet of clingfilm and invert the pastry into a lightly oiled 23 cm/9 inch loose-based flan tin, easing it into the base and sides. Prick the base with a fork, then chill for 1 hour. Place a sheet of baking parchment and baking beans in the case and bake blind in the preheated oven for 10 minutes. Remove the parchment and beans and bake for a further 5 minutes. Remove and cool.

2 To make the filling, heat the chocolate, cream and half the sugar in a saucepan over a low heat, stirring until melted and smooth. Remove from the heat and cool slightly before beating in the egg, egg yolk and crème de cacao. Spread evenly over the pastry base. Cut each pear half crossways into thin slices and arrange over the custard, gently fanning them towards the centre and pressing into the custard. Bake for 10 minutes. Reduce the temperature to 180°C/350°F/Gas Mark 4 and sprinkle the surface evenly with the remaining sugar. Bake for 20–25 minutes until the custard is set and the pears are tender and glazed. Remove from the oven and leave to cool slightly. Serve with spoonfuls of whipped cream.

Ingredients   SERVES 6–8

For the chocolate pastry:
125 g/4 oz unsalted butter, softened
65 g/2½ oz caster sugar
2 tsp vanilla extract
175 g/6 oz plain flour, sifted
40 g/1½ oz cocoa powder
whipped cream, to serve

For the filling:
125 g/4 oz dark chocolate, chopped
225 ml/8 fl oz whipping cream
50 g/2 oz caster sugar
1 large egg
1 large egg yolk
1 tbsp crème de cacao
3 ripe pears, peeled, halved and cored

Helpful Hint
The chocolate pastry is very soft so rolling it between sheets of clingfilm will make it much easier to handle without having to add a lot of extra flour.

Double Chocolate Truffle Slice

1 Preheat the oven to 200˚C/400˚F/Gas Mark 6, 15 minutes before baking. Prepare the chocolate pastry and chill in the refrigerator for 1 hour.

2 Roll the dough out to a rectangle about 38 x 15 cm/15 x 6 inches and use to line a rectangular loose-based flan tin, trim, then chill in the refrigerator for 1 hour.

3 Place a sheet of nonstick baking parchment and baking beans in the pastry case, then bake blind in the preheated oven for 20 minutes. Remove the baking parchment and beans and bake for 10 minutes more. Leave to cool completely.

4 Bring the cream to the boil. Remove from the heat and add the chocolate all at once, stirring until melted and smooth. Beat in the butter, then stir in the brandy or liqueur. Leave to cool slightly, then pour into the cooked pastry shell. Refrigerate until set.

5 Cut out 2.5 cm/1 inch strips of nonstick baking parchment. Place over the tart in a crisscross pattern and dust with icing sugar or cocoa powder. Refrigerate until ready to serve. Leave to soften at room temperature for 15 minutes before serving.

Ingredients   12–14 SLICES

1 quantity chocolate pastry
  (*see* page 36)
300 ml/½ pint double cream
300 g/11 oz dark chocolate, chopped
25–40 g/1–1½ oz unsalted
  butter, diced
50 ml/2 fl oz brandy or liqueur
icing sugar or cocoa powder,
  for dusting

Tasty Tip
Liqueurs that would work very well in this recipe include Tia Maria, Kahlùa, Cointreau, Grand Marnier, Amaretto and Crème de Menthe.

2

4

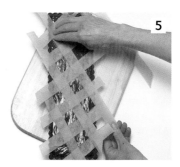

5

Autumn Tart

1 Sift the flour and salt into a bowl or a food processor, add the sugar and butter and rub in or process until the mixture resembles fine crumbs. Add the egg yolk and 1 tablespoon cold water and mix to a dough. Knead until smooth, then wrap in clingfilm and chill for 30 minutes.

2 Preheat the oven to 180°C/350°F/Gas Mark 4 and grease a 20.5 cm/8 inch round flan tin. Roll the pastry out on a lightly floured surface and use to line the tin. Trim the top and reserve the trimmings. Press the pastry into the sides of the tin and prick the base with a fork.

3 To make the filling, put the butter and sugar in a bowl and beat until fluffy. Beat in the ground almonds and egg yolk and spoon into the pastry case. Arrange the sliced fruit over the filling. Mix the lemon juice and caster sugar together and brush over the top of the fruit filling.

4 Roll out the pastry trimmings and cut out leaf shapes and mark veins on. Brush the edge of the tart with milk, place the leaves round the edge and brush with milk. Bake for 30 minutes, or until the pastry is golden and the fruit is tender and golden. Serve with crème fraîche.

Ingredients   SERVES 6–8

175 g/6 oz plain flour
pinch salt
1 tbsp caster sugar
75 g/3 oz butter, diced
1 egg yolk

For the filling:

50 g/2 oz butter
50 g/2 oz caster sugar
50 g/2 oz ground almonds
1 egg yolk
2 dessert apples, peeled, cored
  and sliced
4 plums, pitted and sliced
2 tbsp lemon juice
2 tbsp caster sugar
milk, for brushing
crème fraîche, to serve

Double Chocolate Banoffee Tart

1 Preheat the oven to 190°C/375°F/Gas Mark 5, 10 minutes before baking. Place the milk in a heavy-based saucepan over a gentle heat. Bring to the boil, stirring constantly. Boil gently for about 3–5 minutes until golden. Remove from the heat and leave to cool. To make the crust, place the biscuits with the melted butter, sugar and ginger in a food processor and blend together. Press into the sides and base of a 23 cm/9 inch loose-based flan tin with the back of a spoon. Chill in the refrigerator for 15–20 minutes, then bake in the preheated oven for 5–6 minutes. Remove from the oven and leave to cool.

2 Melt the dark chocolate in a medium saucepan with 150 ml/$^1/_4$ pint of the cream, the syrup and the butter over a low heat. Stir until smooth. Pour into the crumb crust, tilting the tin to distribute the chocolate evenly. Chill in the refrigerator for at least 1 hour until set. Heat 150 ml/$^1/_4$ pint of the remaining cream until hot, then add all the white chocolate and stir until melted and smooth. Stir in the vanilla extract and strain into a bowl. Leave to cool to room temperature. Scrape the cooked condensed milk into a bowl and whisk until smooth, adding a little of the remaining cream if too thick. Spread over the chocolate layer, then slice the bananas and arrange over the top. Whisk the remaining cream until soft peaks form. Stir a spoonful of the cream into the white chocolate mixture, then fold in the remaining cream. Spread over the bananas. Dust with cocoa powder and chill until ready to serve.

Ingredients   SERVES 8

2 x 400 g cans sweetened
  condensed milk
175 g/6 oz dark chocolate, chopped
600 ml/1 pint whipping cream
1 tbsp golden syrup
25 g/1 oz butter, diced
150 g/5 oz white chocolate, grated
  or finely chopped
1 tsp vanilla extract
2–3 ripe bananas
cocoa powder, for dusting

For the ginger crumb crust:
24–26 gingernut biscuits, roughly
  crushed
100 g/3$^1/_2$ oz butter, melted
$^1/_2$ tbsp sugar, or to taste
$^1/_2$ tsp ground ginger

Tasty Tip
Do not assemble the tart more than 2–3 hours before serving as it will go too soft.

2

2

2

Chocolate Apricot Linzer Torte

1 Preheat the oven to 190°C/375°F/Gas Mark 5, 10 minutes before baking. Lightly oil a 28 cm/11 inch flan tin. Place the almonds and half the sugar into a food processor and blend until finely ground. Add the remaining sugar, flour, cocoa powder, cinnamon, salt and orange zest and blend again. Add the diced butter and blend in short bursts to form coarse crumbs. Add the water 1 tablespoon at a time until the mixture starts to come together. Turn onto a lightly floured surface and knead lightly, roll out, then, using your fingertips, press half the dough onto the base and sides of the tin. Prick the base with a fork and chill in the refrigerator. Roll out the remaining dough between two pieces of clingfilm to a 28–30.5 cm/11–12 inch round. Slide the round onto a baking sheet and chill in the refrigerator for 30 minutes.

2 For the filling, spread the apricot jam evenly over the chilled pastry base and sprinkle with the chopped chocolate.

3 Slide the dough round onto a lightly floured surface and peel off the top layer of clingfilm. Using a straight edge, cut it into 1 cm/^{1}/$_2$ inch strips; allow to soften until slightly flexible. Place half the strips, about 1 cm/^{1}/$_2$ inch apart, to create a lattice pattern. Press down on each side of each crossing to accentuate the effect. Press the ends of the strips to the edge, cutting off any excess. Bake for 35 minutes, or until cooked. Leave to cool before dusting with icing sugar and serving.

Ingredients   SERVES 10–12

For the chocolate almond pastry:
75 g/3 oz whole blanched almonds
125 g/4 oz caster sugar
215 g/7^1/$_2$ oz plain flour
2 tbsp cocoa powder
1 tsp ground cinnamon
^{1}/$_2$ tsp salt
grated zest of 1 orange
225 g/8 oz unsalted butter, diced
2–3 tbsp iced water

For the filling:
350 g/12 oz apricot jam
75 g/3 oz milk chocolate, chopped
icing sugar, for dusting

Tasty Tip
When making the pastry, do not allow the dough to form into a ball or it will be tough.

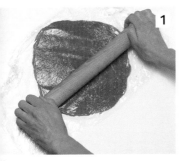

Mini Strawberry Tartlets

1 Sift the flour and icing sugar into a bowl and add the diced butter. Rub the butter into the flour with your fingertips until the mixture resembles fine crumbs. Alternatively, place the flour, icing sugar and butter in a food processor and process until fine crumbs form. Stir in the ground almonds and egg yolk and mix with 1 tablespoon cold water to form a soft dough. Cover with clingfilm and chill for 30 minutes.

2 Preheat the oven to 200°C/400°F/Gas Mark 6 and grease a 12-hole muffin tin. Roll out the dough on a lightly floured surface to 6 mm/¹/₂ inch thickness and cut out twelve 10 cm/4 inch circles. Press the circles into the holes in the tin, loosely fluting up the edges. Prick the bases with a fork and bake for 12–15 minutes until light golden. Leave to cool in the tins for 3 minutes, then remove to cool completely on a wire rack.

3 To make the filling, whip the cream until stiff, then mix with the cream cheese, sugar and liqueur. Chill until needed and then spoon into the pastry cases.

4 Arrange the fresh strawberries on top and brush lightly with a little jam to glaze. Decorate with small fresh mint leaves and serve immediately.

Ingredients   MAKES 12

225 g/8 oz plain flour
25 g/1 oz icing sugar
125 g/4 oz butter, diced
25 g/1 oz ground almonds
1 egg yolk

For the filling:

85 ml/3 fl oz double cream
175 g/6 oz full-fat cream cheese
25 g/1 oz vanilla caster sugar
2 tbsp amaretto almond-flavoured
    liqueur
250 g/9 oz strawberries, hulled, and
    halved if large
2 tbsp raspberry jam, sieved
small mint leaves,
    to decorate

Chocolate Peanut Butter Pie

1 Place the wafers or cookies with the melted butter, sugar and vanilla extract in a food processor and blend together. Press into the base of 23 cm/9 inch pie plate or flat tin. Chill for 15–20 minutes. Place 3 tablespoons of cold water in a bowl and sprinkle over the powdered gelatine; leave until softened.

2 Blend half the caster sugar with the cornflour and salt in a heavy-based saucepan and gradually whisk in the milk. Bring to the boil, then reduce the heat and boil gently for 1–2 minutes until thickened and smooth, stirring constantly. Beat all the yolks together, then add half the hot milk mixture and whisk until blended. Whisk in the remaining milk mixture, return to a clean saucepan and cook gently until it comes to the boil and thickens. Boil, stirring vigorously, for 1 minute, then pour a quarter into a bowl. Add the chopped chocolate and rum or vanilla and stir until melted and smooth. Pour into the chocolate crust and chill in the refrigerator until set.

3 Add the gelatine into the remaining custard and whisk until thoroughly dissolved. Whisk in the peanut butter until melted and smooth. Whisk the egg whites until stiff, then whisk in the remaining sugar, 1 tablespoon at a time. Whip the cream until soft peaks form. Fold 125 ml/4 fl oz of the cream into the custard, then fold in the egg whites. Spread the peanut butter cream mixture over the chocolate layer. Spread or pipe the remaining cream over the surface. Decorate with chocolate curls and chill until ready to serve.

Ingredients   SERVES 8

22–24 chocolate wafers or peanut butter cookies
100 g/3^1/$_2$ oz butter, melted
1–2 tbsp granulated sugar
1 tsp vanilla extract
1^1/$_2$ tbsp powdered gelatine
100 g/3^1/$_2$ oz caster sugar
1 tbsp cornflour
^{1}/$_2$ tsp salt
225 ml/8 fl oz milk
2 large eggs, separated
2 large egg yolks
100 g/3^1/$_2$ oz dark chocolate, chopped
2 tbsp rum or 2 tsp vanilla extract
125 g/4 oz smooth peanut butter
300 ml/^{1}/$_2$ pint whipping cream
chocolate curls, to decorate

Mini Pistachio & Chocolate Strudels

1 Preheat the oven to 170°C/325°F/Gas Mark 3, 10 minutes before baking. Lightly oil 2 large baking sheets. For the filling, mix the finely chopped pistachio nuts, the sugar and dark chocolate in a bowl. Sprinkle with the rosewater and stir lightly together and reserve.

2 Cut each filo pastry sheet into 4 to make 23 x 18 cm/9 x 7 inch rectangles. Place 1 rectangle on the work surface and brush with a little melted butter. Place another rectangle on top and brush with a little more butter. Sprinkle with a little caster sugar and spread about 1 dessertspoon of the filling along one short end. Fold the short end over the filling, then fold in the long edges and roll up. Place on the baking sheet seam-side down. Continue with the remaining pastry sheets and filling until both are used.

3 Brush each strudel with the remaining melted butter and sprinkle with a little caster sugar. Bake in the preheated oven for 20 minutes, or until golden brown and the pastry is crisp.

4 Remove from the oven and leave on the baking sheet for 2 minutes, then transfer to a wire rack. Dust with icing sugar. Place the melted white chocolate in a small piping bag fitted with a plain writing pipe and pipe squiggles over the strudels. Leave to set before serving.

Ingredients   MAKES 24

12 large sheets filo pastry
50 g/2 oz butter, melted
1–2 tbsp caster sugar, for sprinkling
50 g/2 oz white chocolate, melted,
  to decorate

For the filling:
125 g/4 oz unsalted pistachios,
  finely chopped
3 tbsp caster sugar
50 g/2 oz dark chocolate,
  finely chopped
1–2 tsp rosewater
1 tbsp icing sugar, for dusting

Helpful Hint
Keep the unused filo pastry covered with a clean damp tea towel to prevent it from drying out.

'Mars' Bar Mousse in Filo Cups

1 Preheat the oven to 180°C/350 F/Gas Mark 4, 10 minutes before baking. Lightly oil 6 x 150 ml/¹/₄ pint ramekins. Cut the filo pastry into 15 cm/6 inch squares. Place one square on the work surface, brush with a little of the melted butter and sprinkle with a little caster sugar. Butter a second square and lay it over the first at an angle, sprinkle with a little more caster sugar and repeat with two more pastry squares. Press the assembled pastry into the oiled ramekins, pressing into the bases to make flat bottoms and keeping the edges pointing up. Place on a baking sheet and bake in the preheated oven for 10–15 minutes until crisp and golden. Remove and leave to cool before removing the cups from the ramekins. Leave until cold.

2 Place the 'Mars' bars and milk in a small saucepan, stirring until melted and smooth. Leave to cool for 10 minutes, stirring occasionally. Whisk the cream until thick and stir a spoonful into the melted mixture, then fold in the remaining cream. Whisk the egg white until stiff and fold into the mixture together with the cocoa. Chill the mousse for 2–3 hours.

3 For the topping, boil 125 ml/4 fl oz of the whipping cream, add the white chocolate and vanilla extract and stir until smooth. Strain into a bowl and leave to cool. Whisk the remaining cream until thick, then fold into the mixture. Spoon the mousse into the cups, cover with the cream mixture and sprinkle with chocolate. Chill before serving.

Ingredients   MAKES 6

6 large sheets filo pastry, thawed
   if frozen
40 g/1¹/₂ oz unsalted butter, melted
1 tbsp caster sugar
3 x 65 g/2¹/₂ oz 'Mars' bars, coarsely
   chopped
1¹/₂ tbsp milk
300 ml/¹/₂ pint double cream
1 large egg white
1 tsp cocoa powder
1 tbsp dark chocolate, grated

For the topping:
300 ml/¹/₂ pint whipping cream
125 g/4 oz white chocolate, grated
1 tsp vanilla extract

Banoffee Pie

1 Sift the flour and salt into a bowl or a food processor and add the sugar and butter. Rub in or process until the mixture resembles fine crumbs. Add the egg yolk and a few drops of cold water and mix to a dough. Knead until smooth, then wrap in clingfilm and chill for 30 minutes.

2 Preheat the oven to 200°C/400°F/Gas Mark 6 and grease a 20.5 cm/8 inch round flan tin. Roll the pastry out on a lightly floured surface and use to line the tin. Press the pastry into the sides of the tin and prick the base with a fork. Line the pastry case with greaseproof paper and baking beans, bake for 10 minutes, remove the beans, then bake for a further 5–10 minutes until golden. Place the tin on a wire rack to cool.

3 Meanwhile, make the filling. Gently heat the butter and sugar in a small pan until the butter melts and all the grains of sugar dissolve. Bring to the boil, then let boil for 1 minute. Remove from the heat and add the condensed milk and the 2 tablespoons milk. Stir together, then bring back to the boil and let boil for 2 minutes, stirring constantly. Remove from the heat. Place the sliced bananas in the pastry case and pour the warm toffee over. Leave to cool for 1 hour. Whip the cream and spread over the cold banoffee filling. Sprinkle with the grated chocolate and serve immediately.

Ingredients SERVES 6–8

175 g/6 oz plain flour
pinch salt
1 tbsp caster sugar
75 g/3 oz butter, diced
1 egg yolk

For the filling and topping:

75 g/3 oz butter
50 g/2 oz soft light
   brown sugar
225 g/8 oz canned
   condensed milk
2 tbsp milk
3 bananas, peeled and sliced
150 ml/¼ pint double cream
25 g/1 oz plain chocolate, grated,
   to decorate

Raspberry Chocolate Ganache & Berry Tartlets

1 Preheat the oven to 200°C/400°F/Gas Mark 6, 15 minutes before cooking. Make the chocolate pastry and use to line 8 x 7.5 cm/3 inch tartlet tins. Bake blind in the preheated oven for 12 minutes.

2 Place 400 ml/14 fl oz of the cream and half of the raspberry jam in a saucepan and bring to the boil, whisking constantly to dissolve the jam. Remove from the heat and add the chocolate all at once, stirring until the chocolate has melted.

3 Pour into the pastry-lined tartlet tins, shaking gently to distribute the ganache evenly. Chill in the refrigerator for 1 hour, or until set.

4 Place the berries in a large shallow bowl. Heat the remaining raspberry jam with half the framboise liqueur over a medium heat until melted and bubbling. Drizzle over the berries and toss gently to coat. Divide the berries among the tartlets, piling them up if necessary. Chill in the refrigerator until ready to serve.

5 Remove the tartlets from the refrigerator for at least 30 minutes before serving. Using an electric whisk, whisk the remaining cream with the caster sugar and the remaining framboise liqueur until it is thick and softly peaking. Serve with the tartlets and crème fraîche.

Ingredients　　　SERVES 8

1 quantity chocolate pastry (see page 36)
600 ml/1 pint whipping cream
275 g/10 oz seedless raspberry jam
225 g/8 oz dark chocolate, chopped
700 g/1½ lb raspberries or other summer berries
50 ml/2 fl oz framboise liqueur
1 tbsp caster sugar
crème fraîche, to serve

Tasty Tip

Try substituting an equal quantity of white chocolate for the plain chocolate in this recipe, as raspberries go very well with it.

1

2

3

White Chocolate & Macadamia Tartlets

1 Preheat the oven to 200°C/400°F/Gas Mark 6, 15 minutes before baking. Roll the pastry out on a lightly floured surface and use to line 10 x 7.5–9 cm/3–3¹/₂ inch tartlet tins. Line each tin with a small piece of foil and fill with baking beans. Arrange on a baking sheet and bake blind in the preheated oven for 10 minutes. Remove the foil and baking beans and leave to cool.

2 Beat the eggs with the sugar until light and creamy, then beat in the golden syrup, the butter, cream and vanilla or almond extract. Stir in the macadamia nuts. Sprinkle 100 g/3¹/₂ oz of the chopped white chocolate equally over the bases of the tartlet cases and divide the mixture evenly among them.

3 Reduce the oven temperature to 180°C/350°F/Gas Mark 4 and bake the tartlets for 20 minutes, or until the tops are puffy and golden and the filling is set. Remove from the oven and leave to cool on a wire rack.

4 Carefully remove the tartlets from their tins and arrange closely together on the wire rack. Melt the remaining white chocolate and, using a teaspoon or a small paper piping bag, drizzle the melted chocolate over the surface of the tartlets in a zigzag pattern. Serve slightly warm or at room temperature.

Ingredients SERVES 10

1 quantity sweet shortcrust pastry
   (see page 32)
2 medium eggs
50 g/2 oz caster sugar
250 ml/8 fl oz golden syrup
40 g/1¹/₂ oz butter, melted
50 ml/2 fl oz whipping cream
1 tsp vanilla or almond extract
225 g/8 oz unsalted macadamia
   nuts, coarsely chopped
150 g/5 oz white chocolate,
   coarsely chopped

Food Fact

Macadamia nuts come from Hawaii and are large crisp buttery-flavoured nuts. They are readily available from supermarkets.

Lemon Meringue Pie

1 Preheat the oven to 200°C/400°F/Gas Mark 6 and place a baking sheet in it. Sift the flour and salt into a bowl or a food processor and add the fats. Rub in with your fingers or process until the mixture resembles fine crumbs. Mix in 2–3 tablespoons cold water to form a soft dough, then knead lightly until smooth. Grease a 20.5 cm/8 inch round flan tin. Roll out the pastry on a lightly floured surface and use to line the dish. Chill for 30 minutes. Put the zest and granulated sugar in a pan with the water over a low heat and stir until the sugar has completely dissolved. Blend the cornflour with the lemon juice to a smooth paste, then add to the pan and bring to the boil, stirring. Boil for 2 minutes, then remove from the heat and beat in the egg yolks. Set aside to cool.

2 Prick the pastry case, line with greaseproof paper and pour in baking beans. Place on the baking sheet and bake for 10 minutes. Remove from the oven and lift out the paper and beans. Bake for a further 10 minutes. Remove from the oven, spoon the lemon filling into the pastry case and reserve. Reduce the oven temperature to 150°C/300°F/Gas Mark 2.

3 Whisk the egg whites in a clean dry bowl until very stiff. Whisk in half the caster sugar a little at a time, then fold in the remainder. Spread over the filling, covering the top. Bake for 30 minutes until the meringue is golden. Leave to 'settle' for 20 minutes before serving, or eat cold on the day of baking.

Ingredients   SERVES 4–6

175 g/6 oz plain flour
pinch salt
40 g/1^1/$_2$ oz lard or white vegetable
    fat, cut into small pieces
40 g/1^1/$_2$ oz butter or block
    margarine, cut into small pieces

For the filling:

grated zest and juice
    of 2 lemons
75 g/3 oz granulated
    sugar
300 ml/^{1}/$_2$ pint water
40 g/1^1/$_2$ oz cornflour
2 large egg yolks

For the topping:

2 large egg whites
125 g/4 oz caster sugar

Chocolaty Puffs

1 Preheat the oven to 220°C/425°F/Gas Mark 7, 15 minutes before baking. Lightly oil a large baking sheet. To make the choux pastry, sift the flour and cocoa powder together. Place 250 ml/8 fl oz water, the salt, sugar and butter in a saucepan and bring to the boil. Remove from the heat and add the flour mixture, beating vigorously with a wooden spoon until the mixture forms a ball. Return to the heat and cook for 1 minute, stirring, then cool slightly. Using an electric mixer, beat in 4 of the eggs, one at a time, beating well after each addition. Beat the last egg and add a little at a time until the dough is thick and shiny and just falls from a spoon when tapped lightly on the side of the saucepan. Pipe or spoon 12 large puffs onto the baking sheet, leaving space between. Bake for 30–35 minutes until puffy and golden. Remove from the oven, slice off the top third of each bun and return to the oven for 5 minutes to dry out. Remove and leave to cool.

2 For the filling, heat the chocolate with 125 ml/4 fl oz of the double cream and the caster sugar, if using, stirring until smooth, then leave to cool. Whisk the remaining cream until soft peaks form and stir in the crème de cacao, if using. Quickly fold the cream into the chocolate, then spoon or pipe into the choux buns and place the lids on top.

3 Place the sauce ingredients in a small saucepan and heat gently, stirring until smooth. Remove from the heat and leave to cool, stirring occasionally, until thickened. Pour over the puffs and serve.

Ingredients   MAKES 12

For the choux pastry:
150 g/5 oz plain flour
2 tbsp cocoa powder
$^1/_2$ tsp salt
1 tbsp granulated sugar
125 g/4 oz butter, cut into pieces
5 large eggs

For the chocolate cream filling:
225 g/8 oz dark chocolate, chopped
600 ml/1 pint double cream
1 tbsp caster sugar (optional)
2 tbsp crème de cacao (optional)

For the chocolate sauce:
225 g/8 oz dark chocolate
300 ml/$^1/_2$ pint whipping cream
50 g/2 oz butter, diced
1–2 tbsp golden syrup
1 tsp vanilla extract

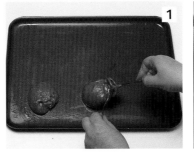

Rice Pudding & Chocolate Tart

1 Preheat the oven to 200°C/400°F/Gas Mark 6, 15 minutes before baking. Roll the chocolate pastry out and use to line a 23 cm/9 inch flan tin. Place a sheet of nonstick baking parchment and baking beans in the tin and bake blind in the preheated oven for 15 minutes.

2 For the ganache, place the cream and golden syrup in a heavy-based saucepan and bring to the boil. Remove from the heat and add the chocolate all at once, stirring until smooth. Beat in the butter and vanilla extract, pour into the baked pastry case and reserve.

3 For the rice pudding, bring the milk and salt to the boil in a medium-size saucepan. Split the vanilla pod and scrape the seeds into the milk and add the vanilla pod. Sprinkle in the rice, then bring to the boil. Reduce the heat and simmer until the rice is tender and the milk is creamy. Remove from the heat.

4 Blend the cornflour and sugar together, then make a paste by stirring in 2 tablespoons water. Stir a little of the hot rice into the cornflour mixture, then stir the cornflour mixture into the rice. Bring to the boil and cook, stirring, until thickened. Set the base of the saucepan into a bowl of iced water and stir until cooled and thickened. Spoon the rice pudding into the tart, smoothing the surface. Leave to set. Dust with cocoa and decorate with fresh mint and blueberries to serve.

Ingredients   SERVES 8

1 quantity chocolate pastry (*see* page 36)
1 tsp cocoa powder, for dusting

For the chocolate ganache:
200 ml/7 fl oz double cream
1 tbsp golden syrup
175 g/6 oz dark chocolate, chopped
1 tbsp butter
1 tsp vanilla extract

For the rice pudding:
1 litre/1³/₄ pints milk
¹/₂ tsp salt
1 vanilla pod
100 g/3¹/₂ oz long-grain white rice
1 tbsp cornflour
2 tbsp granulated sugar

To decorate:
fresh mint sprigs
few fresh blueberries

Classic Apple Strudel

1 Preheat the oven to 190°C/375°F/Gas Mark 5 and butter a large baking sheet. Peel, core and slice the apples, finely grate the zest from the orange and squeeze out the juice. Place the apples, orange zest and juice and caster sugar in a pan and cook over a gentle heat for 10 minutes until the apples are tender, then pour into a bowl, stir in the raisins and leave to cool.

2 Melt 25 g/1 oz of the butter in a nonstick frying pan and add the breadcrumbs. Cook for a minute to brown, then add the almonds and cook for a further minute. Remove from the heat, stir in the cinnamon and leave to cool.

3 Melt the remaining butter and brush 1 large or 2 small filo sheets overlapping. Reserve one sheet for decoration and continue buttering and layering the sheets. Brush the top sheet with butter. Sprinkle over half the breadcrumb mixture, leaving a 5 cm/2 inch border. Top with the cooked apples, then the remaining breadcrumb mixture. Fold in the sides, then roll up to encase the filling. Place on the greased baking sheet seam-side down. Arrange the reserved sheet on top in ruffles and brush the roll all over with butter. Bake for 20–30 minutes until crisp and light golden. Place on a serving dish and dust with icing sugar. Serve sliced with whipped cream, crème fraîche or thick natural yogurt.

Ingredients   SERVES 8

700 g/1½ lb cooking apples
zest and juice of 1 orange
50 g/2 oz natural caster sugar
75 g/3 oz raisins
125 g/4 oz butter
50 g/2 oz fresh white breadcrumbs
40 g/1½ oz flaked almonds
½ tsp ground cinnamon
350 g/12 oz filo pastry sheets
icing sugar, for dusting
whipped cream, crème fraîche or
    natural yogurt, to serve

Chocolate Fruit Pizza

1 Preheat the oven to 200°C/400°F/Gas Mark 6, 15 minutes before baking. Lightly oil a large baking sheet. Roll the prepared pastry out to a 23 cm/9 inch round and place the pastry round onto the baking sheet, and crimp the edges. Using a fork, prick the base all over and chill in the refrigerator for 30 minutes.

2 Line the pastry with foil and weigh down with an ovenproof flat dinner plate or base of a large flan tin and bake blind in the preheated oven until the edges begin to colour. Remove from the oven and discard the weight and foil.

3 Carefully spread the chocolate spread over the pizza base and arrange the peach and nectarine slices around the outside edge in overlapping circles. Toss the berries with the plain chocolate and arrange in the centre. Drizzle with the melted butter and sprinkle with the sugar.

4 Bake in the preheated oven for 10–12 minutes until the fruit begins to soften. Transfer the pizza to a wire rack.

5 Sprinkle the white chocolate and hazelnuts over the surface and return to the oven for 1 minute, or until the chocolate begins to soften. If the pastry starts to darken too much, cover the edge with strips of foil. Remove to a wire rack and leave to cool. Decorate with sprigs of fresh mint and serve warm.

Ingredients   SERVES 8

1 quantity chocolate pastry (see page 36)
2 tbsp chocolate spread
1 small peach, very thinly sliced
1 small nectarine, very thinly sliced
150 g/5 oz strawberries, halved or quartered
75 g/3 oz raspberries
75 g/3 oz blueberries
75 g/3 oz dark chocolate, roughly chopped
1 tbsp butter, melted
2 tbsp granulated sugar
75 g/3 oz white chocolate, chopped
1 tbsp hazelnuts, toasted and chopped
fresh mint sprigs, to decorate

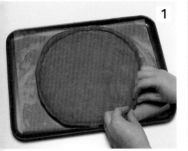
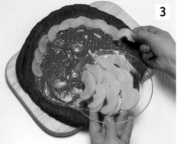

Freeform Fruit Pie

1   Sift the flour into a bowl or a food processor and add the fats, cut into small pieces. Rub in with your fingertips or process until fine crumbs form. Stir in the sugar and the egg yolk and mix with a few drops of cold water to make a soft dough. Knead lightly, then wrap in clingfilm and chill for 30 minutes.

2   Preheat the oven to 190°C/375°F/Gas Mark 5 and grease a large baking sheet. Roll out the pastry to a circle approximately 30 cm/12 inches wide.

3   Lift the pastry onto a rolling pin and place on the baking sheet.

4   Beat the egg yolk and brush this lightly over the pastry. Sprinkle the semolina lightly over the egg yolk.

5   Mix the gooseberries with the sugar and zest and pile into the centre of the pastry circle, leaving a border of 8 cm/3¹/₄ inches all round.

6   Gather the pastry edges up over the filling. Press the edges together roughly, leaving the centre exposed. Beat the egg whites until foaming, then brush over the pastry. Scatter over the caster sugar and bake for about 30 minutes until golden. Remove to a serving plate and serve with vanilla ice cream.

Ingredients   SERVES 6

175 g/6 oz plain flour
40 g/1¹/₂ oz lard or white vegetable fat
40 g/1¹/₂ oz butter
1 tbsp caster sugar
1 medium egg, separated

For the filling:

2 tbsp semolina
600 g/1 lb 5 oz gooseberries
75 g/3 oz caster sugar
zest of 1 orange, finely grated
1 egg, separated
2 tbsp caster sugar
vanilla ice cream, to serve

Chocolate Lemon Tartlets

1 Preheat the oven to 200°C/400°F/Gas Mark 6, 15 minutes before baking. Roll the prepared pastry out on a lightly floured surface and use to line 10 x 7.5 cm/3 inch tartlet tins. Place a small piece of crumpled foil in each and bake blind in the preheated oven for 12 minutes. Remove from the oven and leave to cool.

2 Bring the cream to the boil, then remove from the heat and add the chocolate all at once. Stir until smooth and melted. Beat in the butter and vanilla extract and pour into the tartlets and leave to cool.

3 Beat the lemon curd until soft and spoon a thick layer over the chocolate in each tartlet, spreading gently to the edges. Do not chill in the refrigerator or the chocolate will be too firm.

4 Place the custard sauce into a large bowl and gradually whisk in the cream and almond extract until the custard is smooth and runny.

5 To serve, spoon a little custard onto a plate and place a tartlet in the centre. Sprinkle with grated chocolate and almonds, then serve.

Ingredients   SERVES 4

1 quantity chocolate pastry (*see* page 36)
175 ml/6 fl oz double cream
175 g/6 oz dark chocolate, chopped
2 tbsp butter, diced
1 tsp vanilla extract
350 g/12 oz lemon curd
225 ml/8 fl oz bought custard sauce
225 ml/8 fl oz single cream
$^1/_2$ –1 tsp almond extract

To decorate:

grated chocolate
toasted flaked almonds

Rhubarb & Raspberry Cobbler

1 Preheat the oven to 220°C/425°F/Gas Mark 7. Butter a 1.7 litre/3 pint ovenproof dish.

2 Mix the rhubarb chunks with the raspberries and sugar and place in the buttered dish. Finely grate the zest from the orange and reserve. Squeeze out the juice and add to the dish with the rhubarb. Cover the dish with a piece of foil and bake for 20 minutes.

3 To make the topping, sift the flour and baking powder into a bowl and stir in the grated orange zest. Rub in the butter with your fingertips until the mixture resembles fine crumbs. Stir in the caster sugar and quickly add the milk. Mix with a fork to make a soft dough. (The mixture has to be made quickly, as the raising agent – baking powder – starts to activate as soon as liquid is added.)

4 Take the dish out of the oven and discard the foil. Break off rough tablespoons of the dough and drop them on top of the fruit filling. Bake for about 25 minutes until the topping is firm and golden. Serve immediately with custard or single cream.

Ingredients   SERVES 4

325 g/11½ oz rhubarb, cut into
  chunks
175 g/6 oz raspberries
50 g/2 oz golden caster sugar
zest and juice of 1 orange

For the topping:
225 g/8 oz plain flour
1 tbsp baking powder
50 g/2 oz butter, diced
50 g/2 oz caster sugar

150 ml/¼ pint milk
custard or double cream,
  to serve

Fudgy Mocha Pie with Espresso Custard Sauce

1 Preheat the oven to 180°C/350°F/Gas Mark 4, 10 minutes before baking. Line with foil or lightly oil a deep 23 cm/9 inch pie plate. Melt the chocolate and butter in a small saucepan over a low heat and stir until smooth, then reserve. Dissolve the instant espresso powder in 1–2 tablespoons of hot water and reserve.

2 Beat the eggs with the golden syrup, the sugar, the dissolved espresso powder, the cinnamon and milk until blended. Add the melted chocolate mixture and whisk until blended. Pour into the pie plate.

3 Bake the pie in the preheated oven for about 20–25 minutes until the edge has set but the centre is still very soft. Leave to cool, remove from the plate, then dust lightly with icing sugar.

4 To make the custard sauce, dissolve the instant espresso powder with 2–3 tablespoons of hot water, then whisk into the custard sauce. Slowly add the single cream, whisking constantly, then stir in the coffee-flavoured liqueur, if using. Serve slices of the pie in a pool of espresso custard with strawberries.

Ingredients   SERVES 10

125 g/4 oz dark chocolate, chopped
125 g/4 oz butter, diced
1 tbsp instant espresso powder
4 large eggs
1 tbsp golden syrup
125 g/4 oz granulated sugar
1 tsp ground cinnamon
3 tbsp milk
icing sugar, for dusting
few fresh strawberries, to serve

For the espresso custard sauce:

2–3 tbsp instant espresso
   powder, or to taste
225 ml/8 fl oz bought custard sauce
225 ml/8 fl oz single cream
2 tbsp coffee-flavoured liqueur
   (optional)

Chocolate Pecan Angel Pie

1   Preheat the oven to 110°C/225°F/Gas Mark ¹/₄, 5 minutes before baking. Lightly oil a 23 cm/9 inch pie plate. Using an electric mixer, whisk the egg whites and cream of tartar on a low speed until foamy, then increase the speed and beat until soft peaks form. Gradually beat in the sugar, 1 tablespoon at a time, beating well after each addition, until stiff glossy peaks form and the sugar is completely dissolved. (If still gritty, continue beating.) This will take about 15 minutes. Beat in 2 teaspoons of the vanilla extract, then fold in the nuts and the chocolate chips.

2   Spread the meringue in the pie plate, making a shallow well in the centre and slightly building up the sides. Bake in the oven for 1–1¹/₄ hours until a golden creamy colour. Lower the temperature if it colours too quickly. Turn the oven off, but do not remove the meringue. Leave the oven door ajar (about 5 cm/2 inches) for about 1 hour. Transfer to a wire rack until cold.

3   Pour the cream into a small saucepan and bring to the boil. Remove from the heat, add the grated white chocolate and stir until melted. Add the remaining vanilla extract and leave to cool, then whip until thick. Spoon the whipped cream into the pie shell, piling it high and swirling decoratively. Decorate with fresh raspberries and chocolate curls. Chill in the refrigerator for 2 hours before serving. When ready to serve, add sprigs of mint on the top and cut into slices.

Ingredients   SERVES 8–10

4 large egg whites
¹/₄ tsp cream of tartar
225 g/8 oz caster sugar
3 tsp vanilla extract
100 g/3¹/₂ oz pecans, lightly toasted and chopped
75 g/3 oz dark chocolate chips
150 ml/¹/₄ pint double cream
150 g/5 oz white chocolate, grated

To decorate:
fresh raspberries
dark chocolate curls
few fresh mint sprigs

Helpful Hint
The meringue needs to be cooked gently at a low temperature and then allowed to cool in the oven so that it can become crisp and dry without cracking too much.

White Chocolate Mousse & Strawberry Tart

1 Preheat the oven to 200°C/400°F/Gas Mark 6, 15 minutes before baking. Roll the prepared pastry out on a lightly floured surface and use to line a 25.5 cm/10 inch flan tin. Line with either kitchen foil or nonstick baking parchment and baking beans, then bake blind in the oven for 15–20 minutes. Remove the foil or parchment and return to the oven for a further 5 minutes.

2 To make the mousse, place the white chocolate with 2 tablespoons water and 125 ml/4 fl oz of the cream in a saucepan and heat gently, stirring until melted and smooth. Remove from the heat, stir in the kirsch or framboise liqueur and cool. Whip the remaining cream until soft peaks form. Fold a spoonful of the cream into the cooled white chocolate mixture, then fold in the remaining cream. If using, whisk the egg whites until stiff and gently fold into the white chocolate cream mixture to make a softer, lighter mousse. Chill in the refrigerator for 15–20 minutes.

3 Heat the jam with the kirsch or framboise liqueur and brush or spread half the mixture onto the pastry base. Leave to cool. Spread the chilled mousse over the jam and arrange the strawberries in concentric circles over the top. If necessary, reheat the jam and glaze the strawberries lightly. Chill the tart for about 3–4 hours until the mousse has set. Serve.

Ingredients   10 SLICES

1 quantity sweet shortcrust pastry
   (see page 32)

For the white chocolate mousse:

250 g/9 oz white chocolate, chopped
350 ml/12 fl oz double cream
3 tbsp kirsch or framboise liqueur
1–2 large egg whites (optional)

65 g/2$\frac{1}{2}$ oz strawberry jam
1–2 tbsp kirsch or framboise liqueur
450–700 g/1–1$\frac{1}{2}$ lb ripe
   strawberries, sliced lengthways

Helpful Hint

This recipe contains raw egg whites, which should be eaten with caution by vulnerable groups including the elderly, young and pregnant women. If you are worried, omit them from the recipe.

Apple Pie

1 Sift the flour and salt into a bowl or a food processor and add the fats, cut into small pieces. Rub in with your fingertips or process until the mixture resembles fine crumbs. Mix in the sugar and add 2–3 tablespoons cold water to form a soft dough, then knead lightly until smooth. Wrap and chill for 30 minutes.

2 Preheat the oven to 220°C/425°F/Gas Mark 7 and grease a 1.2 litre/2¼ pint deep pie dish. Roll out the pastry on a lightly floured surface. Turn the pie dish upside down onto the pastry and cut round it to form the lid. Roll the trimmings into a 2.5 cm/1 inch strip and press this firmly onto the top edge of the dish.

3 Mix the sliced apples with the sugar, spices and sultanas. Place in the dish and then dot with butter. Dampen the pastry edge with water, then place the pastry lid over. Press the edges to seal, and flute together with your thumb and forefinger. Make a hole in the centre to allow the steam to escape, then decorate with pastry trimmings.

4 Brush with milk, then sprinkle with caster sugar. Bake for 10 minutes, then turn the oven temperature down to 190°C/375°F/Gas Mark 5 and bake for a further 25–30 minutes until crisp and golden. Serve hot straight away with cream or custard.

Ingredients   SERVES 6–8

175 g/6 oz plain flour
pinch salt
40 g/1½ oz lard or white vegetable fat
40 g/1½ oz butter or block margarine
1 tbsp caster sugar

For the filling:

500 g/1 lb 1 oz cooking apples, peeled, cored and sliced
125 g/4 oz caster sugar
1 tsp ground cinnamon
½ tsp ground nutmeg
50 g/2 oz sultanas
15 g/½ oz butter
milk, for glazing
caster sugar, for sprinkling

cream or custard, to serve

Chocolate Raspberry Mille Feuille

1 Preheat the oven to 200°C/400°F/Gas Mark 6, 15 minutes before baking. Lightly oil a large baking sheet and sprinkle with a little water. Roll out the pastry on a lightly floured surface to a rectangle about 43 x 28 cm/17 x 11 inches. Cut into three long strips. Mark each strip crossways at 6.5 cm/ 2½ inch intervals using a sharp knife. Carefully transfer to the baking sheet, keeping the edges as straight as possible. Bake for 20 minutes, or until well risen and golden brown. Place on a wire rack and leave to cool. Carefully transfer each rectangle to a work surface and, using a sharp knife, trim the long edges straight. Cut along the knife marks to make 18 rectangles.

2 Place all the sauce ingredients in a food processor and blend until smooth. If the purée is too thick, add a little water. Adjust the sweetness if necessary. Strain into a bowl, cover and chill.

3 Place one rectangle on the work surface flat-side down, spread with a little ganache and sprinkle with a few raspberries. Spread a second rectangle with ganache, place over the first, pressing gently, then sprinkle with raspberries. Place a third rectangle on top, flat-side up, and spread with ganache. Arrange some raspberries on top and dust lightly with a little icing sugar. Repeat with the remaining pastry rectangles, chocolate ganache and fresh raspberries. Chill in the refrigerator until required and serve with the raspberry sauce and any remaining fresh raspberries.

Ingredients   SERVES 6

450 g/1 lb puff pastry, thawed if frozen
1 quantity chocolate raspberry ganache (see page 56), chilled
700 g/1½ lb fresh raspberries, plus extra for decorating
icing sugar, for dusting

For the raspberry sauce:
225 g/8 oz fresh raspberries
2 tbsp seedless raspberry jam
1–2 tbsp caster sugar, or to taste
2 tbsp lemon juice or framboise liqueur

Helpful Hint
Marking the uncooked pastry makes cutting the baked pastry easier and neater. But if you prefer, make one big mille feuille by leaving the three strips whole at the end of step 1. Slice the finished mille feuille with a sharp serrated knife.

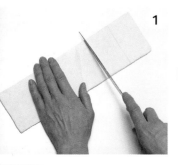

1

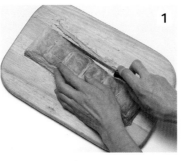

1

3

Caramelised Chocolate Tartlets

1 Preheat the oven to 200°C/400°F/Gas Mark 6, 15 minutes before baking. Lightly oil six individual tartlet tins. Roll out the ready-made pastry on a lightly floured surface and use to line the oiled tins. Prick the bases and sides with a fork and line with nonstick baking parchment and baking beans. Bake blind for 10 minutes in the preheated oven, then remove from the oven and discard the baking beans and the baking parchment.

2 Reduce the oven temperature to 180°C/350°F/Gas Mark 4. Heat the coconut milk and 15 g/^{1}/$_2$ oz of the sugar in a heavy-based saucepan, stirring constantly, until the sugar has dissolved. Remove the saucepan from the heat and leave to cool.

3 Stir the melted chocolate, the beaten egg and the vanilla extract into the cooled coconut milk. Stir until well mixed, then strain into the cooked pastry cases. Place on a baking sheet and bake in the oven for 25 minutes, or until set. Remove and leave to cool, then chill in the refrigerator.

4 Preheat the grill, then arrange the fruits in a decorative pattern on the top of each tartlet. Sprinkle with the remaining demerara sugar and place the tartlets in the grill pan. Grill for 2 minutes, or until the sugar bubbles and browns. Turn the tartlets, if necessary, and take care not to burn the sugar. Remove from the grill and leave to cool before serving.

Ingredients — SERVES 6

350 g/12 oz ready-made shortcrust pastry, thawed if frozen
150 ml/1^1/$_4$ pint coconut milk
40 g/1^1/$_2$ oz demerara sugar
50 g/2 oz dark chocolate, melted
1 medium egg, beaten
few drops vanilla extract
1 small mango, peeled, stoned and sliced
1 small papaya, peeled, deseeded and chopped
1 star fruit, sliced
1 kiwi, peeled and sliced, or use fruits of your choice

Helpful Hint

Before grilling, you may find it useful to cover the edges of the pastry with foil to prevent it burning under the hot grill.

1
3

4

Chocolate Profiteroles

1   Preheat the oven to 220°C/425°F/Gas Mark 7, 15 minutes before cooking. Lightly oil two baking sheets. For the pastry, place the water and the butter in a heavy-based saucepan and bring to the boil. Remove from the heat and beat in the flour. Return to the heat and cook for 1 minute, or until the mixture forms a ball. Remove from the heat and leave to cool slightly, then gradually beat in the eggs a little at a time, beating well after each addition. Once all the eggs have been added, beat until the paste is smooth and glossy. Pipe or spoon 20 small balls onto the baking sheets, allowing plenty of room for expansion. Bake in the preheated oven for 25 minutes, or until well risen and golden brown. Reduce the oven temperature to 180°C/350°F/Gas Mark 4. Make a hole in each ball and continue to bake for a further 5 minutes. Remove from the oven and leave to cool.

2   For the custard, place the milk and nutmeg in a heavy-based saucepan and bring to the boil. In another pan, whisk together the yolks, sugar and the flours, then beat in the hot milk. Bring to the boil and simmer, whisking constantly for 2 minutes. Cover and leave to cool. Spoon the custard into the profiteroles and arrange on a large serving dish. Place all the sauce ingredients in a small saucepan and bring to the boil, then simmer for 10 minutes. Remove from the heat and cool slightly before serving with the profiteroles.

Ingredients   SERVES 4

For the pastry:
150 ml/¼ pint water
50 g/2 oz butter
65 g/2½ oz plain flour, sifted
2 medium eggs, lightly beaten

For the custard:
300 ml/½ pint milk
pinch freshly grated nutmeg
3 medium egg yolks
50 g/2 oz caster sugar
2 tbsp plain flour, sifted
2 tbsp cornflour, sifted

For the sauce:
175 g/6 oz soft brown sugar
150 ml/¼ pint boiling water
1 tsp instant coffee
1 tbsp cocoa powder
1 tbsp brandy
75 g/3 oz butter
1 tbsp golden syrup

Easy Danish Pastries

1 Sift the flour and salt into a bowl, add 50 g/2 oz of the butter and rub in until the mixture resembles fine crumbs, then stir in the yeast and sugar. Stir in the milk and beaten eggs and mix to a soft dough. Knead for 10 minutes until smooth. Cover with oiled clingfilm and leave for about 1 hour in a warm place until doubled in size. Place on a floured surface and knead to knock out the air for about 4 minutes until smooth. Roll out into a rectangle 20 x 35 cm/8 x 14 inches. Dot two thirds with half the remaining butter. Fold the plain third up over the buttered section, then fold the top third over to form a parcel. Press the edges to seal, then turn the dough, with the fold to the left. Roll out again to a rectangle and dot with the remaining butter as before. Chill for 15 minutes, then roll out and fold again. Roll, fold and chill once more.

2 Preheat the oven to 220°C/425°F/Gas Mark 7. Roll out the dough into a 55 cm/22 inch square and cut into 16 squares. Put 25 g/1 oz of the grated almond paste or marzipan in the centre of each. Cut the corners of 8 of the squares almost to the middle and fold over the alternate points. Top each of the rest with an apricot half and fold the opposite corners over. Arrange on buttered baking sheets and leave to rise for 20 minutes until puffy. Brush with egg and bake for 15 minutes until golden. When cold, mix the icing sugar with enough water to make a smooth icing. Drizzle over the pastries and place a cherry half on the windmill shapes. Scatter the apricot-filled pastries with flaked almonds and leave to set for 30 minutes.

Ingredients   MAKES 16

500 g/1 lb 1 oz strong white flour
$^1/_2$ tsp salt
350 g/12 oz butter
7 g sachet fast-action yeast
50 g/2 oz caster sugar
150 ml/$^1/_4$ pint lukewarm milk
2 medium eggs, beaten

For the filling and topping:
225 g/8 oz home-made almond
    paste or marzipan, grated
8 canned apricot halves, drained
1 egg, beaten
125 g/4 oz fondant icing sugar
50 g/2 oz glacé cherries, halved
50 g/2 oz flaked almonds

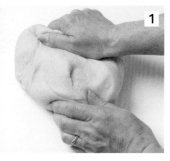

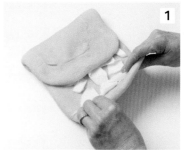

Almond & Pine Nut Tart

1 Preheat the oven to 200°C/400°F/Gas Mark 6. Roll out the pastry and use to line a 23 cm/9 inch fluted flan tin. Chill in the refrigerator for 10 minutes, then line with greaseproof paper and baking beans and bake blind in the preheated oven for 10 minutes. Remove the paper and beans and bake for a further 10–12 minutes until cooked. Leave to cool. Reduce the temperature to 190°C/375°F/Gas Mark 5.

2 Grind the almonds in a food processor until fine. Add the sugar, salt, eggs, vanilla and almond extract and blend. Add the butter, flour and baking powder and blend until smooth.

3 Spread a thick layer of the raspberry jam over the cooled pastry case, then pour in the almond filling. Sprinkle the pine nuts evenly over the top and bake for 30 minutes until firm and browned.

4 Remove the tart from the oven and leave to cool. Dust generously with icing sugar and serve cut into wedges with whipped cream.

Ingredients   SERVES 6

250 g/9 oz ready-made sweet
    shortcrust pastry
75 g/3 oz blanched almonds
75 g/3 oz caster sugar
pinch salt
2 medium eggs
1 tsp vanilla extract
2–3 drops almond extract
125 g/4 oz unsalted butter, softened
2 tbsp flour
$^1/_2$ tsp baking powder
3–4 tbsp raspberry jam
50 g/2 oz pine nuts
icing sugar, to decorate
whipped cream, to serve

Cannoli with Ricotta Cheese

1 Beat together the butter and the sugar until light and fluffy. Add the white wine and salt and mix together well. Fold in the flour and knead to form a soft dough. Reserve for 2 hours.

2 Lightly flour a work surface and roll the dough out to a thickness of about $^1/_2$ cm/$^1/_4$ inch. Cut into 12.5 cm/5 inch squares. Wrap the pastry around the cannoli or cream horn moulds using the beaten egg to seal. Make 3–4 at a time.

3 Heat the vegetable oil to 180°C/350°F in a deep-fat fryer and fry the cannoli for 1–2 minutes until puffed and golden. Drain well on absorbent kitchen paper and leave to cool. Remove the moulds when the cannoli are cool enough to handle. Repeat until all the cannoli are cooked.

4 Beat the ricotta cheese with the sugar, orange water and vanilla extract until creamy. Add the cherries, angelica, candied peel and chopped chocolate. Fill each cannoli using a piping bag with a large plain nozzle or a small spoon. Dust with icing sugar and serve cool, but not cold.

Ingredients   MAKES 24

For the pastry:
25 g/1 oz butter
25 g/1 oz caster sugar
3 tbsp dry white wine
pinch salt
150 g/5 oz plain flour
1 medium egg, lightly beaten
vegetable oil, for deep frying

For the filling:
450 g/1 lb ricotta cheese
125 g/4 oz caster sugar
2 tbsp orange water
1 tsp vanilla extract
50 g/2 oz glacé cherries, chopped
50 g/2 oz angelica, chopped
125 g/4 oz candied peel, chopped
75 g/3 oz dark chocolate, finely
    chopped
icing sugar, for dusting

Biscuits & Bitesize

Individually sized morsels of deliciousness are all the more easily scoffed, or taken to work as an exciting snack. This section has a wide choice of classic biscuits and cookies, alongside a few buns, flapjacks and macaroons. There are good old Chocolate Chip Cookies and Gingerbread Biscuits, fun Traffic Lights biscuits, Classic Flapjacks, adventurous Chocolate Madeleines and cosmopolitan Cantuccini.

Almond & Pistachio Biscotti

1 Preheat the oven to 180°C/350°F/Gas Mark 4. Line a large baking sheet with nonstick baking parchment. Toast the ground almonds and whole nuts lightly and reserve until cool.

2 Beat together the eggs, egg yolk and icing sugar until thick, then beat in the flour, baking powder and salt. Add the lemon zest, ground almonds and whole nuts and mix to form a slightly sticky dough.

3 Turn the dough on to a lightly floured surface and, using lightly floured hands, form into a log measuring approximately 30 cm/12 inches long. Place down the centre of the prepared baking sheet and transfer to the preheated oven. Bake for 20 minutes.

4 Remove from the oven and increase the oven temperature to 200°C/400°F/Gas Mark 6. Cut the log diagonally into 2.5 cm/1 inch slices. Return to the baking sheet, cut-side down, and bake for a further 10–15 minutes until golden, turning once after 10 minutes. Leave to cool on a wire rack and store in an airtight container.

Ingredients   MAKES 12

125 g/4 oz ground almonds
50 g/2 oz shelled pistachios
50 g/2 oz blanched almonds
2 medium eggs
1 medium egg yolk
125 g/4 oz icing sugar
225 g/8 oz plain flour
1 tsp baking powder
pinch salt
zest of $^{1}/_{2}$ lemon

Tasty Tip

These biscuits are also delicious made with a single kind of nut – try hazelnuts or just almonds. When toasting nuts, spread them out on a baking sheet, then place in a preheated oven at 200°C/400°F/Gas Mark 6. Leave for 5–10 minutes, stirring occasionally. If using a lower temperature, leave for a few more minutes.

1   2   4

Chocolate Chip Cookies

1 Preheat the oven to 180°C/350°F/Gas Mark 4, 10 minutes before baking. Lightly butter three or four large baking sheets with 15 g/¹/₂ oz of the butter. Place the remaining butter and both sugars in a food processor and blend until smooth. Add the egg and vanilla extract and blend briefly. Alternatively, cream the butter and sugars together in a bowl, then beat in the egg with the vanilla extract.

2 If using a food processor, scrape out the mixture with a spatula and place the mixture into a large bowl. Sift the flour and bicarbonate of soda together, then fold into the creamed mixture. When the mixture is blended thoroughly, stir in the chocolate chips.

3 Drop heaped teaspoons of the mixture onto the prepared baking sheets, spaced well apart, and bake the cookies in the preheated oven for 10–12 minutes until lightly golden.

4 Leave to cool for a few seconds, then, using a spatula, transfer to a wire rack and cool completely. The cookies are best eaten when just cooked, but can be stored in an airtight container for a few days.

Ingredients   MAKES 30

130 g/4¹/₂ oz butter
50 g/2 oz caster sugar
65 g/2¹/₂ oz soft dark brown sugar
1 medium egg, beaten
¹/₂ tsp vanilla extract
125 g/4 oz plain flour
¹/₂ tsp bicarbonate of soda
150 g/5 oz plain or milk
   chocolate chips

Helpful Hint

For light-textured, crumbly biscuits, do not overwork the biscuit dough. Handle as little as possible and fold the ingredients together gently in a figure of 8 using a metal spoon or rubber spatula. To ring the changes with these basic biscuits, use an equal mixture of chocolate chips and nuts. Alternatively, replace the chocolate chips entirely with an equal quantity of your favourite chopped nuts.

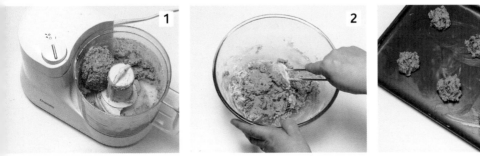

Chewy Choc & Nut Cookies

1   Preheat the oven to 180°C/350°F/Gas Mark 4, 10 minutes
before baking. Lightly butter several baking sheets with the
butter and line with a sheet of nonstick baking parchment.
Place the egg whites in a large grease-free bowl and whisk with
an electric mixer until the egg whites are very frothy.

2   Add the sugar with the cocoa powder, the flour and coffee
powder and whisk again until the ingredients are blended
thoroughly. Add 1 tablespoon water and continue to whisk on
the highest speed until the mixture is very thick. Fold in
the chopped walnuts.

3   Place tablespoons of the mixture onto the prepared baking
sheets, leaving plenty of space between them as they expand
greatly during cooking.

4   Bake in the preheated oven for 12–15 minutes until the tops
are firm, golden and quite cracked. Leave to cool for 30
seconds, then, using a spatula, transfer to a wire rack and leave
to cool. Store in an airtight tin.

Ingredients   MAKES 18

15 g/¹⁄₂ oz butter
4 medium egg whites
350 g/12 oz icing sugar
75 g/3 oz cocoa powder
2 tbsp plain flour
1 tsp instant coffee powder
125 g/4 oz walnuts, finely chopped

Tasty Tip
Although the walnuts in these biscuits
are excellent, hazelnuts or mixed nuts
would also go very well with both the
chocolate and the coffee flavours.

Food Fact
When the Spanish brought the cocoa
bean home, they also brought the word
'cacao' as well. In every other European
country it is still known as cacao – it is
only in English that it is known as cocoa.

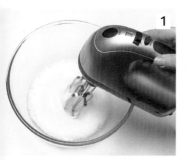

1

2

2

Cherry Garlands

1   Preheat the oven to 190°C/375°F/Gas Mark 5 and grease two baking sheets. Sift the flour and salt into a bowl or a food processor, add the butter and rub in with fingertips or process until the mixture resembles fine crumbs. Stir in the sugar.

2   In another bowl, beat the egg yolk with the almond extract and add to the flour mixture. Stir to make a soft dough, then knead lightly. Roll the dough into pea-size balls and arrange 8 balls in a ring on a baking sheet, pressing them together lightly.

3   Continue making rings until all the dough is used up. Cut each glacé cherry into 8 tiny wedges and place 3 on each biscuit between the balls.

4   Bake for 14 minutes until golden, remove the biscuits from the oven and brush with beaten egg white. Sprinkle the tops lightly with caster sugar and return to the oven for 2 minutes until a sparkly glaze has formed. Leave to stand on the baking sheets for 2 minutes, then cool completely on a wire rack.

Ingredients   MAKES 30

125 g/4 oz plain flour
pinch salt
65 g/2^1/$_2$ oz butter, softened
50 g/2 oz caster sugar
1 egg yolk
^{1}/$_2$ tsp almond extract

To decorate:
12 glacé cherries
1 egg white, lightly beaten
caster sugar

White Chocolate Cookies

1 Preheat the oven to 180°C/350°F/Gas Mark 4, 10 minutes before baking. Lightly butter several baking sheets with 15 g/$^1/_2$ oz of the butter. Place the remaining butter with both sugars into a large bowl and beat with a wooden spoon or an electric mixer until soft and fluffy.

2 Beat the egg, then gradually beat into the creamed mixture. Sift the flour and the bicarbonate of soda together, then carefully fold into the creamed mixture with a few drops of vanilla extract.

3 Roughly chop the chocolate and hazelnuts into small pieces, add to the bowl and gently stir into the mixture. Mix together lightly to blend.

4 Spoon heaped teaspoons of the mixture onto the prepared baking sheets, making sure that there is plenty of space in between each one, as they will spread a lot during cooking.

5 Bake the cookies in the preheated oven for 10 minutes or until golden, then remove from the oven and leave to cool for 1 minute. Using a spatula, carefully transfer to a wire rack and leave to cool completely. The cookies are best eaten on the day they are made. Store in an airtight container.

Ingredients   MAKES 24

130 g/4$^1/_2$ oz butter
40 g/1$^1/_2$ oz caster sugar
65 g/2$^1/_2$ oz soft dark brown sugar
1 medium egg
125 g/4 oz plain flour
$^1/_2$ tsp bicarbonate of soda
few drops vanilla extract
150 g/5 oz white chocolate
50 g/2 oz whole hazelnuts, shelled

Helpful Hint

White chocolate is available in bars as well as in chips. As there are no cocoa solids in white chocolate, look for one with a good percentage of cocoa butter, as it is the cocoa butter that gives the chocolate its luscious creamy texture.

Gingerbread Biscuits

1 Preheat the oven to 180°C/350°F/Gas Mark 4 and grease two baking sheets. Sift the flour, spices and bicarbonate of soda into a bowl.

2 Place the butter, syrup, treacle and sugar in a heavy-based pan with 1 tablespoon water and heat gently until every grain of sugar has dissolved and the butter has melted. Cool for 5 minutes, then pour the melted mixture into the dry ingredients and mix to a soft dough.

3 Leave the dough, covered, for 30 minutes. Roll out the dough on a lightly floured surface to a 3 mm/$\frac{1}{8}$ inch thickness and cut out fancy shapes. Gather up the trimmings and re-roll the dough, cutting out more shapes. Place on the baking sheets using a palette knife and bake for about 10 minutes until golden and firm. Be careful not to overcook, as the biscuits will brown quickly.

4 Decorate the biscuits by mixing the royal icing sugar with enough water to make a piping consistency. Place the icing in a small paper piping bag with the end snipped away and pipe faces and decorations onto the biscuits.

Ingredients

MAKES 20 LARGE OR
28 SMALL BISCUITS

225 g/8 oz plain flour, plus extra
    for dusting
$\frac{1}{2}$ tsp ground ginger
$\frac{1}{2}$ tsp mixed spice
$\frac{1}{2}$ tsp bicarbonate of soda
75 g/3 oz butter
2 tbsp golden syrup
1 tbsp black treacle
75 g/3 oz soft dark
    brown sugar
50 g/2 oz royal icing sugar,
    to decorate

2

2

3

Chocolate Shortcakes

1 Preheat the oven to 170°C/325°F/Gas Mark 3, 10 minutes before baking. Lightly oil several baking sheets and line with nonstick baking parchment. Place the butter, icing sugar and vanilla extract together in a food processor and blend briefly until smooth. Alternatively, using a wooden spoon, cream the butter, icing sugar and vanilla extract in a large bowl.

2 Sift the flour, cocoa powder and salt together, then either add to the food processor bowl and blend quickly to form a dough, or add to the bowl and, using your hands, mix together until a smooth dough is formed. Turn the dough out onto a clean board lined with clingfilm. Place another sheet of clingfilm over the top and roll the dough out until it is 1 cm/$\frac{1}{2}$ inch thick. Transfer the whole board to the refrigerator and chill for 1$\frac{1}{2}$–2 hours.

3 Remove the top piece of clingfilm and use a 5 cm/2 inch cutter to cut the dough into 30–32 rounds. Place the rounds on the prepared baking sheets and bake in the preheated oven for about 15 minutes until firm.

4 Melt the chocolate in a heatproof bowl set over a saucepan of simmering water. Using a spoon or piping bag, drizzle the chocolate over the biscuits. Using a spatula, carefully remove the shortcakes from the baking parchment and transfer to a wire rack. Leave to cool completely. Sprinkle the shortcakes with sifted icing sugar before serving. Store in an airtight container for a few days.

Ingredients   MAKES 30–32

225 g/8 oz unsalted butter, softened
150 g/5 oz icing sugar
1 tsp vanilla extract
250 g/9 oz plain flour
25 g/1 oz cocoa powder
$\frac{1}{2}$ tsp salt
75 g/3 oz milk chocolate,
   to decorate

Food Fact

Using icing sugar instead of caster sugar helps to give these biscuits a really crumbly texture. Do make sure that you use butter rather than margarine to ensure that you get the classic shortbread texture.

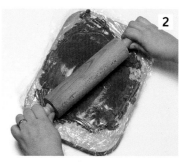

Chocolate Macaroons

1 Preheat the oven to 180°C/350°F/Gas Mark 4, 10 minutes before baking. Lightly oil several baking sheets and line with sheets of nonstick baking parchment. Melt the chocolate in a heatproof bowl set over a saucepan of simmering water. Alternatively, melt in the microwave according to the manufacturer's instructions. Stir until smooth, then cool slightly.

2 Place the ground almonds in a food processor and add the sugar, almond extract, cocoa powder and 1 of the egg whites. Add the melted chocolate and a little of the other egg white and blend to make a soft smooth paste. Alternatively, place the ground almonds with the sugar, almond extract and cocoa powder in a bowl and make a well in the centre. Add the melted chocolate with sufficient egg white and gradually blend together to form a smooth but not sticky paste.

3 Shape the dough into small balls the size of large walnuts and place them on the prepared baking sheets. Flatten them slightly, then brush with a little water. Sprinkle over a little icing sugar and bake in the preheated oven for 10–12 minutes until just firm.

4 Using a spatula, carefully lift the macaroons off the baking parchment and transfer to a wire rack to cool. These are best served immediately, but can be stored in an airtight container.

Ingredients

MAKES 20

65 g/2½ oz plain dark chocolate
125 g/4 oz ground almonds
125 g/4 oz caster sugar
¼ tsp almond extract
1 tbsp cocoa powder
2 medium egg whites
1 tbsp icing sugar

Helpful Hint

If you prefer, you could bake these biscuits on edible rice paper, available from the baking section of supermarkets. Cover the baking sheet with rice paper and drop the mixture onto the paper as directed in the method. Bake in the preheated oven, then tear the paper to release the macaroons.

Coconut Macaroons

1 Preheat the oven to 180°C/350°F/Gas Mark 4. Line two baking sheets with rice paper.

2 Whisk the egg whites in a clean dry bowl until soft peaks form. Using a large metal spoon, fold in the icing sugar. Fold in the coconut, almonds and lemon or lime zest until a sticky dough forms.

3 Heap dessertspoonfuls of the mixture onto the rice paper on the baking sheets. Bake for 10 minutes, then reduce the oven temperature to 150°C/300°F/Gas Mark 2.

4 Bake for a further 5–8 minutes until firm and golden, then remove to a wire rack to cool, breaking off any excess rice paper.

Ingredients   MAKES 18

rice paper
2 medium egg whites
125 g/4 oz icing sugar
125 g/4 oz desiccated coconut
125 g/4 oz ground almonds
zest of $1/2$ lemon or lime,
    finely grated

Chocolate & Ginger Florentines

1 Preheat the oven to 180°C/350°F/Gas Mark 4, 10 minutes before baking. Lightly oil several baking sheets. Melt the butter, cream and sugar together in a saucepan and bring slowly to the boil. Remove from the heat and stir in the almonds and the glacé ginger.

2 Leave to cool slightly, then mix in the flour and the salt. Blend together, then place heaped teaspoons of the mixture on the baking sheets. Make sure they are spaced well apart, as they expand during cooking. Flatten them slightly with the back of a wet spoon.

3 Bake in the preheated oven for 10–12 minutes until just brown at the edges. Leave to cool slightly. Using a spatula, carefully transfer the Florentines to a wire rack and leave to cool.

4 Melt the chocolate in a heatproof bowl set over a saucepan of gently simmering water. Alternatively, melt the chocolate in the microwave according to the manufacturer's instructions, until just liquid and smooth. Spread thickly over one side of the Florentines, then mark wavy lines through the chocolate using a fork and leave until firm.

Ingredients   MAKES 14–16

40 g/1½ oz butter
5 tbsp double cream
50 g/2 oz caster sugar
65 g/2½ oz chopped almonds
25 g/1 oz flaked almonds
40 g/1½ oz glacé ginger, chopped
25 g/1 oz plain flour
pinch salt
150 g/5 oz plain dark chocolate

Melting Moments

1 Preheat the oven to 180°C/350°F/Gas Mark 4. Grease two baking sheets.

2 Beat the butter until light and fluffy, then whisk in the caster sugar and vanilla extract. Sift the flour and salt into the bowl. Add the egg and mix to a soft dough.

3 Break the dough into 16 pieces and roll each piece into a ball. Spread the oats out on a small bowl or plate. Roll each ball in the oats to coat them all over without flattening them.

4 Place a cherry quarter in the centre of each ball, then place on the baking sheets, spaced well apart. Bake for about 15 minutes until risen and golden. Remove from the baking sheets with a palette knife and cool on a wire rack.

Ingredients
MAKES 16

125 g/4 oz butter, softened
75 g/3 oz caster sugar
$1/2$ tsp vanilla extract
150 g/5 oz self-raising flour
pinch salt
1 small egg or $1/2$ medium egg, beaten
25 g/1 oz porridge oats
4 glacé cherries, quartered

Italian Biscotti

1   Preheat the oven to 190°C/375°F/Gas Mark 5, 10 minutes
    before baking. Lightly oil three to four baking sheets and
    reserve. Cream the butter and sugar together in a bowl and
    mix in the vanilla extract. When it is light and fluffy, beat in
    the egg with the cinnamon, lemon zest and the ground
    almonds. Stir in the flour to make a firm dough.

2   Knead lightly until smooth and free from cracks. Shape the
    dough into rectangular blocks about 4 cm/1½ inches in
    diameter, wrap in greaseproof paper and chill in the
    refrigerator for at least 2 hours.

3   Cut the chilled dough into 5 mm/¼ inch slices, place on the
    baking sheets and cook in the preheated oven for 12–15
    minutes until firm. Remove from the oven, cool slightly, then
    transfer to wire racks to cool.

4   When completely cold, melt the chocolate in a heatproof
    bowl set over a saucepan of simmering water. Alternatively,
    melt the chocolate in the microwave according to the
    manufacturer's instructions. Spoon into a piping bag and
    pipe over the biscuits. Leave to dry on a sheet of nonstick
    baking parchment before serving.

Ingredients   MAKES 26–28

150 g/5 oz butter
200 g/7 oz caster sugar
¼ tsp vanilla extract
1 small egg, beaten
¼ tsp ground cinnamon
grated zest of 1 lemon
15 g/½ oz ground almonds
150 g/5 oz plain flour
150 g/5 oz plain dark chocolate

Food Fact

In Italy, these deliciously crunchy little
biscuits are traditionally served with
a sweet dessert wine called Vin Santo.

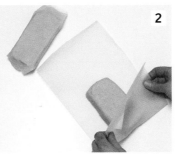

Chocolate & Nut Refrigerator Biscuits

1 Cream 150 g/5 oz of the butter and both sugars in a large bowl until light and fluffy, then gradually beat in the egg.

2 Sift the flour, bicarbonate of soda and cocoa powder together, then gradually fold into the creamed mixture together with the chopped pecans. Mix thoroughly until a smooth but stiff dough is formed.

3 Place the dough on a lightly floured surface or pastry board and roll into sausage shapes about 5 cm/2 inches in diameter. Wrap in clingfilm and chill in the refrigerator for at least 12 hours, or preferably overnight.

4 Preheat the oven to 190°C/375°F/Gas Mark 5, 10 minutes before baking. Lightly grease several baking sheets with the remaining butter. Cut the dough into thin slices and place on the prepared baking sheets. Bake in the preheated oven for 8–10 minutes until firm. Remove from the oven and leave to cool slightly. Using a spatula, transfer to a wire rack to cool. Store in an airtight container.

Ingredients   MAKES 18

165 g/5^1/$_2$ oz slightly salted butter
150 g/5 oz soft dark brown sugar
25 g/1 oz granulated sugar
1 medium egg, beaten
200 g/7 oz plain flour
^{1}/$_2$ tsp bicarbonate of soda
25 g/1 oz cocoa powder
125 g/4 oz pecan nuts,
   finely chopped

Helpful Hint

This dough will keep in the refrigerator for 4–5 days if well wrapped. Cut off and bake a few biscuits as required. When oiling or greasing baking sheets for biscuits, be careful about how much oil or butter you use, especially if using nonstick baking sheets. Very rich mixtures, that use a high proportion of fat, will not need to be baked on oiled baking sheets. If they are, there is the probability that the biscuits will spread too much.

Traffic Lights

1 Preheat the oven to 180°C/350°F/Gas Mark 4. Grease two baking sheets. Beat the butter, sugar and syrup together until light and fluffy.

2 Gradually beat in the egg and vanilla extract. Sift the flour and baking powder into the bowl and stir into the mixture. Gather the mixture up with your hands and work it into a dough. Turn out onto a floured surface and knead gently until smooth. Wrap in clingfilm for 30 minutes and chill.

3 Roll the pastry out to a thickness of 3 mm/$\frac{1}{8}$ inch and cut into 28 oblongs measuring 3 x 8.5 cm/1$\frac{1}{4}$ x 3$\frac{1}{2}$ inches. Using the broad end of a piping nozzle or a cutter measuring 2 cm/$\frac{3}{4}$ inch wide, cut out three holes in each of 14 of the oblongs, remove the cut-out discs and discard or re-roll to use as pastry trimmings. Place all the oblongs on the baking sheets and bake for 8–10 minutes until golden. Transfer to a wire rack to cool.

4 Place 3 small teaspoonfuls of different coloured jams along the centre of each rectangular biscuit, starting with strawberry for red at the top, apricot for amber in the middle and lime marmalade for green at the bottom. Dust the biscuits with the round holes with icing sugar. Position these over the jam on the rectangular biscuits and press down so that the jam shows through.

Ingredients   MAKES 14

125 g/4 oz butter, softened
75 g/3 oz caster sugar
25 g/1 oz golden syrup
1 medium egg, beaten
few drops vanilla extract
275 g/10 oz plain flour, plus
   extra for dusting
1 tsp baking powder

To decorate:

4 tbsp strawberry jam
4 tbsp apricot jam
4 tbsp lime marmalade
icing sugar, for dredging

Chocolate & Hazelnut Cookies

1. Preheat the oven to 180°C/350°F/Gas Mark 4,10 minutes before baking. Lightly oil and flour two to three baking sheets. Chop 25 g/1 oz of the hazelnuts and reserve. Blend the remaining hazelnuts with the caster sugar in a food processor until finely ground. Add the butter to the processor bowl and blend until pale and creamy.

2. Add the salt, cocoa powder and the double cream and mix well. Scrape the mixture into a bowl using a spatula, and stir in the egg whites. Sift the flour, then stir into the mixture together with the rum.

3. Spoon heaped tablespoons of the batter onto the baking sheets and sprinkle over a few of the reserved hazelnuts. Bake in the preheated oven for 5–7 minutes until firm. Remove the cookies from the oven and leave to cool for 1–2 minutes. Using a spatula, transfer to wire racks and leave to cool.

4. When the biscuits are cold, melt the chocolate in a heatproof bowl set over a saucepan of simmering water. Stir until smooth, then drizzle a little of the chocolate over the top of each biscuit. Leave to dry on a wire rack before serving.

Ingredients　　　MAKES 12

75 g/3 oz blanched hazelnuts
100 g/3½ oz caster sugar
50 g/2 oz unsalted butter
pinch salt
5 tsp cocoa powder
3 tbsp double cream
2 large egg whites
40 g/1½ oz plain flour
2 tbsp rum
75 g/3 oz white chocolate

Helpful Hint

Be careful not to chop the hazelnuts for too long in the food processor, as this tends to make them very oily. To blanch hazelnuts or any nut, simply place on a baking sheet and heat in a hot oven for 10 minutes. Remove, then place in a clean tea towel and rub off the brown skins. Do not rub too many at a time, otherwise they may escape from the tea towel.

Chocolate & Almond Biscuits

1 Preheat the oven to 200°C/400°F/Gas Mark 6, 15 minutes before baking. Lightly oil several baking sheets. Cream the butter and icing sugar together until light and fluffy, then gradually beat in the egg, beating well after each addition. When all the egg has been added, stir in the milk and lemon zest.

2 Sift the flour, then stir into the mixture together with the chopped almonds to form a smooth and pliable dough. Wrap in clingfilm and chill in the refrigerator for 2 hours.

3 Roll the dough out on a lightly floured surface, in a large oblong about 5 mm/^{1}/$_4$ inch thick. Cut into strips, about 6.5 cm/2^1/$_2$ inches long and 4 cm/1^1/$_2$ inches wide and place on the prepared baking sheets.

4 Bake in the preheated oven for 15 minutes, or until golden, then remove from the oven and leave to cool for a few minutes. Transfer to a wire rack and leave to cool completely.

5 Melt the chocolate in a heatproof bowl set over a saucepan of simmering water. Alternatively, melt the chocolate in the microwave according to the manufacturer's instructions, until smooth. Spread the chocolate thickly over the biscuits, sprinkle over the toasted flaked almonds and leave to set before serving.

Ingredients   MAKES 18–20

130 g/4^1/$_2$ oz butter
65 g/2^1/$_2$ oz icing sugar
1 medium egg, beaten
1 tbsp milk
grated zest of 1 lemon
250 g/9 oz plain flour
100 g/3^1/$_2$ oz blanched almonds, chopped
125 g/4 oz plain dark chocolate
75 g/3 oz flaked almonds, toasted

Tasty Tip

As an alternative to flaked almonds for decorating these biscuits, use slivered almonds. They are easy to make; simply cut whole blanched almonds into thin slivers.

Fig & Chocolate Bars

1 Preheat the oven to 180°C/350°F/Gas Mark 4, 10 minutes before baking. Lightly oil an 18 cm/7 inch square cake tin. Place the butter and the flour in a large bowl and, using your fingertips, rub the butter into the flour until it resembles fine breadcrumbs.

2 Stir in the sugar, then, using your hand, bring the mixture together to form a dough. Knead until smooth, then press the dough into the prepared tin. Lightly prick the base with a fork and bake in the preheated oven for 20–30 minutes until golden. Remove from the oven and leave the shortbread to cool in the tin until completely cold.

3 Meanwhile, place the dried figs, lemon juice, 125 ml/4 fl oz water and the ground cinnamon in a saucepan and bring to the boil. Cover and simmer for 20 minutes, or until soft, stirring occasionally during cooking. Cool slightly, then purée in a food processor until smooth. Cool, then spread over the cooked shortbread.

4 Melt the chocolate in a heatproof bowl set over a saucepan of simmering water. Alternatively, melt the chocolate in the microwave according to the manufacturer's instructions. Stir until smooth, then spread over the top of the fig filling. Leave to become firm, then cut into 12 bars and serve.

Ingredients   MAKES 12

125 g/4 oz butter
150 g/5 oz plain flour
50 g/2 oz soft light brown sugar
225 g/8 oz ready–to–eat dried figs, halved
juice of ¹/₂ large lemon
1 tsp ground cinnamon
125 g/4 oz plain dark chocolate

Helpful Hint

If you are unable to find ready–to–eat figs, soak dried figs in boiling water for 20 minutes until plump. Drain well and use as above.

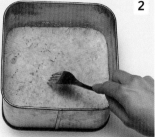

Classic Flapjacks

1 Preheat the oven to 160°C/325°F/Gas Mark 3. Butter a 20.5 cm/8 inch square baking tin.

2 Place the butter, sugar and golden syrup in a saucepan and heat gently until the butter has melted and every grain of sugar has dissolved.

3 Remove from the heat and stir in the oats and vanilla extract. Stir well and then spoon the mixture into the prepared tin.

4 Smooth level with the back of a large spoon. Bake in the centre of the oven for 30–40 minutes until golden. Leave to cool in the tin for 10 minutes, then mark into fingers and leave in the tin until completely cold. When cold, cut into fingers with a sharp knife.

Ingredients MAKES 12

175 g/6 oz butter, plus extra
   for greasing
125 g/4 oz demerara sugar
2 tbsp golden syrup
175 g/6 oz jumbo
   porridge oats
few drops vanilla extract

Chocolate-covered Flapjacks

1 Preheat the oven to 180°C/ 350°F/Gas Mark 4, 10 minutes before baking. Lightly oil a 33 x 23 cm/13 x 9 inch Swiss roll tin and line with nonstick baking parchment. Place the flour, rolled oats, the light muscovado sugar, bicarbonate of soda and salt into a bowl and stir together well.

2 Melt the butter and golden syrup together in a heavy-based saucepan and stir until smooth, then add to the oat mixture and mix together thoroughly. Spoon the mixture into the prepared tin, press down firmly and level the top.

3 Bake in the preheated oven for 15–20 minutes until golden. Remove from the oven and leave the flapjack to cool in the tin. Once cool, remove from the tin. Discard the parchment.

4 Melt the chocolate in a heatproof bowl set over a saucepan of gently simmering water. Alternatively, melt the chocolate in the microwave according to the manufacturer's instructions. Once the chocolate has melted, quickly beat in the cream, then pour over the flapjack. Mark patterns over the chocolate with a fork when almost set.

5 Chill the flapjack in the refrigerator for at least 30 minutes before cutting into bars. When the chocolate has set, serve. Store in an airtight container for a few days.

Ingredients

MAKES 24

215 g/7½ oz plain flour
150 g/5 oz rolled oats
225 g/8 oz light muscovado sugar
1 tsp bicarbonate of soda
pinch salt
150 g/5 oz butter
2 tbsp golden syrup
250 g/9 oz plain dark chocolate
5 tbsp double cream

Helpful Hint

Try lightly oiling your measuring spoon before dipping it into the golden syrup. The syrup will slide off the spoon easily. Alternatively, warm the syrup slightly before measuring.

Shortbread Thumbs

1 Preheat the oven to 150°C/300°F/Gas Mark 2, 10 minutes before baking. Lightly oil two baking sheets. Sift the flour into a large bowl, cut 75 g/3 oz of the butter and the white vegetable fat into small cubes, add to the flour, then, using your fingertips, rub in until the mixture resembles fine breadcrumbs.

2 Stir in the granulated sugar, sifted cornflour and 4 tablespoons of the cocoa powder and bring the mixture together with your hand to form a soft and pliable dough.

3 Place on a lightly floured surface and shape into 12 small balls. Place onto the baking sheets at least 5 cm/2 inches apart, then press each one with a clean thumb to make a dent.

4 Bake in the preheated oven for 20–25 minutes until light golden brown. Remove from the oven and leave for 1–2 minutes to cool. Transfer to a wire rack and leave until cold.

5 Sift the icing sugar and the remaining cocoa powder into a bowl and add the remaining softened butter. Blend to form a smooth and spreadable icing with 1–2 tablespoons hot water. Spread a little icing over the top of each biscuit and place half a cherry on each. Leave until set before serving.

Ingredients   MAKES 12

125 g/4 oz self-raising flour
125 g/4 oz butter, softened
25 g/1 oz white vegetable fat
50 g/2 oz granulated sugar
25 g/1 oz cornflour, sifted
5 tbsp cocoa powder, sifted
125 g/4 oz icing sugar
6 assorted coloured glacé cherries,
    rinsed, dried and halved

Helpful Hint

After baking, remove the cooked biscuits as soon as possible from the baking sheets as they will continue to cook and could overcook. Cool completely on wire cooling racks before storing in airtight containers.

Food Fact

Using a combination of butter and vegetable fat gives these biscuits a softer texture than using all butter.

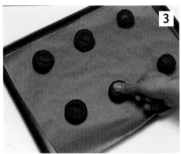

Golden Honey Fork Biscuits

1 Preheat the oven to 180°C/350°F/Gas Mark 4. Grease two baking sheets.

2 Place the butter and sugar in a bowl and beat together until light and fluffy. Beat in the egg, a little at a time, and then beat in the vanilla extract and honey.

3 Sift the flour, baking powder and cinnamon into the bowl and fold into the mixture with a large metal spoon.

4 Put heaped teaspoons of the mixture onto the prepared baking sheets, leaving room for them to spread out during baking. Press the top of each round with the tines of a fork to make a light indentation.

5 Bake for 10–12 minutes until golden. Cool for 2 minutes on the baking sheets, then transfer to a wire rack to cool completely.

Ingredients   MAKES 20–24

125 g/4 oz butter or block
    margarine, diced
125 g/4 oz soft light
    brown sugar
1 medium egg, beaten
$^1/_2$ tsp vanilla extract
2 tbsp clear honey
200 g/7 oz plain flour
$^1/_2$ tsp baking powder
$^1/_2$ tsp ground cinnamon

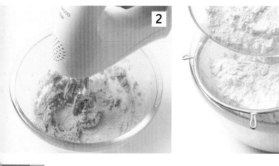

Chequered Biscuits

1 Preheat the oven to 190°C/375°F/Gas Mark 5, 10 minutes before baking. Lightly oil three to four baking sheets. Place the butter and icing sugar in a bowl and cream together until light and fluffy.

2 Add the salt, then gradually add the flour, beating well after each addition. Mix well to form a firm dough. Cut the dough in half and knead the cocoa powder into one half. Wrap both portions of dough separately in clingfilm and then leave to chill in the refrigerator for 2 hours.

3 Divide each piece of dough into three portions. Roll each portion of dough into a long roll and arrange these rolls on top of each other to form a chequerboard design, sealing them with egg white. Wrap in clingfilm and refrigerate for 1 hour.

4 Cut the dough into 5 mm/1/4 inch thick slices, place on the baking sheets and bake in the preheated oven for 10–15 minutes. Remove from the oven and leave to cool for a few minutes. Transfer to a wire rack and leave until cold before serving. Store in an airtight container.

Ingredients   MAKES 20

150 g/5 oz butter
75 g/3 oz icing sugar
pinch salt
200 g/7 oz plain flour
25 g/1 oz cocoa powder
1 small egg white

Food Fact
Recipes for sweet biscuits and pastries often contain a pinch of salt. This helps to enhance the sweet flavour without making it savoury.

Coconut & Almond Munchies

1 Preheat the oven to 150°C/300°F/Gas Mark 2, 10 minutes before baking. Line several baking sheets with rice paper. Place the egg whites in a clean, grease-free bowl and whisk until stiff and standing in peaks. Sift the icing sugar, then carefully fold half of the sugar into the whisked egg whites together with the ground almonds. Add the coconut, the remaining icing sugar and the lemon zest and mix together to form a very sticky dough.

2 Place the mixture in a piping bag and pipe into walnut-size mounds onto the rice paper, then sprinkle with a little extra icing sugar. Bake in the preheated oven for 20–25 minutes until set and golden on the outside. Remove from the oven and leave to cool slightly. Using a spatula, carefully transfer to a wire rack and leave until cold.

3 Break the milk and white chocolate into pieces and place in two separate bowls. Melt both chocolates set over saucepans of gently simmering water. Alternatively, melt in the microwave according to the manufacturer's instructions. Stir until smooth and free from lumps. Dip one edge of each munchie in the milk chocolate and leave to dry on nonstick baking parchment. When dry, dip the other side into the white chocolate. Leave to set, then serve as soon as possible.

Ingredients   MAKES 26–30

5 medium egg whites
250 g/9 oz icing sugar, plus extra
   to sprinkle
225 g/8 oz ground almonds
200 g/7 oz desiccated coconut
grated zest of 1 lemon
125 g/4 oz milk chocolate
125 g/4 oz white chocolate

Helpful Hint

You could, if preferred, drop spoonfuls of this mixture onto the rice paper. However, piping the dough ensures that the munchies will be more evenly sized.

 1

 2

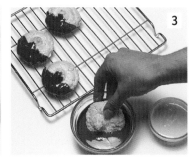 3

Honey & Chocolate Hearts

1 Preheat the oven to 220°C/425°F/Gas Mark 7, 15 minutes before baking. Lightly oil two baking sheets. Heat the sugar, butter and honey together in a small saucepan until everything has melted and the mixture is smooth.

2 Remove from the heat and stir until slightly cooled, then add the beaten egg with the salt and beat well. Stir in the mixed peel or glacé ginger, ground cinnamon, ground cloves, the flour and the baking powder and mix well until a dough is formed. Wrap in clingfilm and chill in the refrigerator for 45 minutes.

3 Place the chilled dough on a lightly floured surface, roll out to about 5 mm/¼ inch thickness and cut out small heart shapes. Place onto the prepared baking sheets and bake in the preheated oven for 8–10 minutes. Remove from the oven and leave to cool slightly. Using a spatula, transfer to a wire rack to cool.

4 Melt the chocolate in a heatproof bowl set over a saucepan of simmering water. Alternatively, melt the chocolate in the microwave according to the manufacturer's instructions, until smooth. Dip one half of each biscuit in the melted chocolate. Leave to set before serving.

Ingredients   MAKES 20

65 g/2½ oz caster sugar
15 g/½ oz butter
125 g/4 oz thick honey
1 small egg, beaten
pinch salt
1 tbsp mixed peel or chopped glacé ginger
¼ tsp ground cinnamon
pinch ground cloves
225 g/8 oz plain flour, sifted
½ tsp baking powder, sifted
75 g/3 oz milk chocolate

Tasty Tip

Try different types of honey to vary the flavour of the biscuits. Acacia honey, for example, is very mild, while heather honey has a more pronounced flavour.

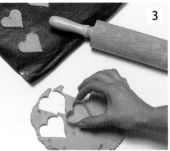

Chocolate Orange Biscuits

1 Preheat the oven to 200°C/400°F/Gas Mark 6, 15 minutes before baking. Lightly oil several baking sheets. Coarsely grate the chocolate and reserve. Beat the butter and sugar together until creamy. Add the salt, beaten egg and half the orange zest and beat again.

2 Sift the flour and baking powder, add to the bowl with the grated chocolate and beat to form a dough. Shape into a ball, wrap in clingfilm and chill in the refrigerator for 2 hours.

3 Roll the dough out on a lightly floured surface to 5 mm/¹⁄₄ inch thickness and cut into 5 cm/2 inch rounds. Place the rounds on the prepared baking sheets, allowing room for expansion. Bake in the preheated oven for 10–12 minutes until firm. Remove the biscuits from the oven and leave to cool slightly. Using a spatula, transfer to a wire rack and leave to cool.

4 Sift the icing sugar into a small bowl and stir in sufficient orange juice to make a smooth, spreadable icing. Spread or pipe the icing over the biscuits, leave until almost set, then sprinkle on the remaining grated orange zest before serving.

Ingredients   MAKES 30

100 g/3¹⁄₂ oz plain dark chocolate
125 g/4 oz butter
125 g/4 oz caster sugar
pinch salt
1 medium egg, beaten
grated zest of 2 oranges
200 g/7 oz plain flour
1 tsp baking powder
125 g/4 oz icing sugar
1–2 tbsp orange juice

Helpful Hint

To get the maximum amount of juice from citrus fruits, heat the whole fruit in the microwave for about 40 seconds, then cool slightly before squeezing. Alternatively, roll the fruit on the table, pressing lightly before squeezing out the juice. It is important to add the orange juice gradually to the icing mixture because you may not need all of it to obtain a spreadable consistency.

Rum & Chocolate Squares

1 Preheat the oven to 190°C/375°F/Gas Mark 5, 10 minutes before baking. Lightly oil several baking sheets. Cream the butter, sugar and salt together in a large bowl until light and fluffy. Add the egg yolks and beat well until smooth.

2 Sift together 175 g/6 oz of the flour, the cornflour and the baking powder and add to the mixture and mix well with a wooden spoon until a smooth and soft dough is formed.

3 Halve the dough and knead the cocoa powder into one half and the rum and the remaining plain flour into the other half. Place the two mixtures in two separate bowls, cover with clingfilm and chill in the refrigerator for 1 hour.

4 Roll out both pieces of dough separately on a well-floured surface into two thin rectangles. Place one on top of the other, cut out squares approximately 5 cm x 5 mm/ 2 inches x ¼ inch and place on the prepared baking sheets.

5 Bake in the preheated oven, half with the chocolate uppermost and the other half rum side up, for 10–12 minutes until firm. Remove from the oven and leave to cool slightly. Using a spatula, transfer to a wire rack and leave to cool, then serve.

Ingredients   MAKES 14–16

125 g/4 oz butter
100 g/3½ oz caster sugar
pinch salt
2 medium egg yolks
225 g/8 oz plain flour
50 g/2 oz cornflour
¼ tsp baking powder
2 tbsp cocoa powder
1 tbsp rum

Tasty Tip

If you prefer, you could substitute rum flavouring for the rum in this recipe. However, you would need to reduce the amount to about 1 teaspoon.

Viennese Fingers

1 Preheat the oven to 180°C/350°F/Gas Mark 4. Grease two baking sheets. Put the butter and icing sugar in a bowl and beat together until soft and fluffy.

2 Whisk in the egg and vanilla extract with 1 tablespoon of the flour. Sift in the remaining flour and the baking powder and beat with a wooden spoon to make a soft dough.

3 Place the mixture in a piping bag fitted with a large star nozzle and pipe into 6.5 cm/2^1/$_2$ inch lengths on the baking sheets. Bake for 15–20 minutes until pale golden and firm, then transfer to a wire rack to cool.

4 When cold, thinly spread one flat side of a biscuit with apricot jam and sandwich together with another biscuit.

5 To decorate the biscuits, break the chocolate into squares and place in a heatproof bowl and stand this over a pan of simmering water. Stir until the chocolate has melted, then dip the ends of the biscuits into the chocolate to coat. Leave on a wire rack for 1 hour until set.

Ingredients   MAKES 28

225 g/8 oz butter, softened
75 g/3 oz icing sugar
1 medium egg, beaten
1 tsp vanilla extract
275 g/10 oz plain flour
^{1}/$_2$ tsp baking powder

To decorate:
4 tbsp sieved apricot jam
225 g/8 oz plain chocolate

Chocolate Whirls

1. Preheat the oven to 180°C/350°F/Gas Mark 4, 10 minutes before baking. Lightly oil two baking sheets. Cream the margarine, butter and icing sugar together until the mixture is light and fluffy.

2. Stir the chocolate until smooth, then beat into the creamed mixture. Stir in the cornflour. Sift the flours together, then gradually add to the creamed mixture, a little at a time, beating well after each addition. Beat until the consistency is smooth and stiff enough for piping.

3. Put the mixture in a piping bag fitted with a large star nozzle and pipe 40 small whirls onto the prepared baking sheets.

4. Bake the whirls in the preheated oven for 12–15 minutes until firm to the touch. Remove from the oven and leave to cool for about 2 minutes. Using a spatula, transfer the whirls to wire racks and leave to cool.

5. Meanwhile, make the buttercream. Cream the butter with the vanilla extract until soft. Gradually beat in the icing sugar and add a little cooled boiled water if necessary, to give a smooth consistency. When the whirls are cold, pipe or spread on the prepared buttercream, sandwich together and serve.

Ingredients   MAKES 20

125 g/4 oz soft margarine
75 g/3 oz unsalted butter, softened
75 g/3 oz icing sugar, sifted
75 g/3 oz plain dark chocolate, melted and cooled
15 g/$^{1}/_{2}$ oz cornflour, sifted
125 g/4 oz plain flour
125 g/4 oz self-raising flour

For the buttercream:
125 g/4 oz unsalted butter, softened
$^{1}/_{2}$ tsp vanilla extract
225 g/8 oz icing sugar, sifted

Helpful Hint
It is important that the fats are at room temperature and the flours are sifted. Do not put too much mixture into the piping bag. If liked, the buttercream can be replaced with whipped cream, but the whirls should be eaten on the day they are filled.

Chocolate & Vanilla Rings

1   Preheat the oven to 180°C/350°F/Gas Mark 4 and grease two baking sheets.

2   Put the butter and sugar in a bowl and beat until light and fluffy. Add the vanilla extract, sift in the flour and mix to a soft dough. Divide the dough in two and add the cocoa powder to one half and the almonds to the other.

3   Knead each piece of dough separately into a smooth ball, wrap and chill for 30 minutes. Divide each piece into 26 pieces. Take one dark and one light ball and roll each separately into ropes about 12.5 cm/5 inches long using your fingers.

4   Twist the ropes together to form a circlet and pinch the ends together. Repeat with the remaining dough and place on a greased baking sheet. Bake for 12–14 minutes until risen and firm. Remove to cool on a wire rack.

Ingredients   MAKES 26

175 g/6 oz butter, softened
125 g/4 oz caster sugar
few drops vanilla extract
250 g/9 oz plain flour
15 g/$^1/_2$ oz cocoa powder
25 g/1 oz ground almonds

2

3

4

Chocolate Madeleines

1 Preheat the oven to 180°C/350°F/Gas Mark 4, 10 minutes before baking. Lightly oil ten dariole moulds and line the bases of each with a small circle of nonstick baking parchment. Stand the moulds on a baking tray. Cream the butter and sugar together until light and fluffy. Gradually add the eggs, beating well after each addition. Beat in the almond extract and ground almonds.

2 Sift the flour, cocoa powder and baking powder over the creamed mixture. Gently fold in using a metal spoon. Divide the mixture equally between the prepared moulds; each should be about half full.

3 Bake on the centre shelf of the preheated oven for 20 minutes, or until well risen and firm to the touch. Leave in the tins for a few minutes, then run a small palette knife round the edges and turn out onto a wire rack to cool. Remove the paper circles from the sponges.

4 Heat the conserve with the liqueur, brandy or juice in a small saucepan. Sieve to remove any lumps. If necessary, trim the sponge bases, so they are flat. Brush the tops and sides with warm conserve, then roll in the coconut. Top each with a chocolate button, fixed by brushing its base with conserve.

Ingredients   MAKES 10

125 g/4 oz butter
125 g/4 oz soft light brown sugar
2 medium eggs, lightly beaten
1 drop almond extract
1 tbsp ground almonds
75 g/3 oz self-raising flour
20 g/³/₄ oz cocoa powder
1 tsp baking powder

To finish:
5 tbsp apricot conserve
1 tbsp amaretto liqueur, brandy or
   orange juice
50 g/2 oz desiccated coconut
10 large chocolate buttons (optional)

Helpful Hint
Oil the tins well and, if liked, dust with a little flour, shaking off any excess flour. Place a small circle of nonstick baking parchment in the bases before filling, to make removing the cooked cakes easier. Remove soon after baking, as they have a tendency to stick.

Chocolate Chelsea Buns

1 Preheat the oven to 190°C/375°F/Gas Mark 5, 10 minutes before baking. Lightly oil an 18 cm/7 inch square tin. Place the pears in a bowl with the fruit juice, stir, then cover and leave to soak while making the dough.

2 Sift the flour, cinnamon and salt into a bowl, rub in 25 g/1 oz of the butter, then stir in the yeast and make a well in the middle. Add the milk and egg and mix to a soft dough. Knead on a floured surface for 10 minutes until smooth and elastic, then place in a bowl. Cover with clingfilm and leave in a warm place to rise for 1 hour, or until doubled in size.

3 Turn out on a lightly floured surface and knead the dough lightly before rolling out to a rectangle, about 30.5 x 23 cm/ 12 x 9 inches. Melt the remaining butter and brush over. Spoon the pears and chocolate evenly over the dough, leaving a 2.5 cm/1 inch border, then roll up tightly, starting at a long edge. Cut into twelve equal slices, then place cut-side up in the tin. Cover and leave to rise for 25 minutes, or until doubled in size.

4 Bake on the centre shelf of the preheated oven for 30 minutes, or until well risen and golden brown. Cover with foil after 20 minutes if the filling is starting to brown too much. Remove from the oven and brush with the maple syrup while hot, then leave in the tin for 10 minutes to cool slightly. Turn out onto a wire rack and leave to cool. Separate the buns and serve warm.

Ingredients   MAKES 12

75 g/3 oz dried pears, finely chopped
1 tbsp apple or orange juice
225 g/8 oz strong plain flour
1 tsp ground cinnamon
$^1/_2$ tsp salt
40 g/1$^1/_2$ oz butter
1$^1/_2$ tsp easy-blend dried yeast
125 ml/4 fl oz warm milk
1 medium egg, lightly beaten
75 g/3 oz plain dark chocolate, chopped
3 tbsp maple syrup

Tasty Tip

As an alternative, replace the pears and juice with an equal weight of chopped hazelnuts or almonds.

Hot Cross Buns

1   Sift the flour, salt and mixed spice into a bowl and then stir in the sugar and yeast. In a jug, whisk together the milk and the egg. Add the liquid to the flour in the bowl with the cooled melted butter and mix to a soft dough. Knead for 10 minutes until smooth and elastic. Knead in the fruit and then place the dough in a bowl. Cover it with oiled clingfilm. Leave in a warm place for about 1 hour until doubled in size. Butter a large 32 x 23 cm/12 x 9 inch baking tray or a roasting tin. Cut the dough into 12 chunks and roll each one into a ball. Place in the tray, leaving enough space for the buns to rise and spread out. Cover with the oiled clingfilm and leave for about 45 minutes until doubled in size.

2   Preheat the oven to 200°C/400°F/Gas Mark 6. Discard the clingfilm and brush the buns with the beaten egg. Roll the pastry into long thin strips. Place a pastry strip over and along the length of each bun, then place another strip in the opposite direction to make crosses. Repeat, topping all the buns with pastry crosses. Bake for 20–25 minutes until risen and golden.

3   Heat 2 tablespoons water and add the caster sugar, continuing to heat gently until the sugar is completely dissolved. While still hot, turn the buns out of the tray and place on a wire rack. Brush the sugar glaze over the warm buns and leave to cool. These are best eaten on the day of baking. Split and toast any leftovers and serve with butter.

Ingredients   MAKES 12

500 g/1 lb 1 oz strong white
    bread flour
1 tsp salt
2 tsp mixed spice
50 g/2 oz soft light
    brown sugar
7 g sachet fast-action
    dried yeast
275 ml/9 fl oz milk
1 medium egg, beaten
50 g/2 oz butter, melted
    and cooled
225 g/8 oz mixed dried fruit

For the decoration:
1 medium egg, beaten
75 g/3 oz shortcrust pastry
50 g/2 oz caster sugar

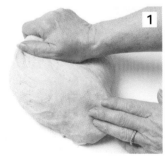

Drop Scones

1   Grease a heavy-based nonstick frying pan or a flat griddle pan with white vegetable fat and heat gently.

2   Sift the flour and baking powder into a bowl, stir in the sugar and make a well in the centre. Add the egg and half the milk and beat to a smooth thick batter. Beat in enough of the remaining milk to give the consistency of thick cream.

3   Drop the mixture onto the hot pan 1 heaped tablespoon at a time, spacing them well apart. When small bubbles rise to the surface of each scone, flip them over with a palette knife and cook for about 1 minute until golden brown.

4   Place on a serving dish and keep warm, covered with a clean cloth, while you cook the remaining mixture. Serve warm with butter and syrup and eat on the day of making.

Ingredients   MAKES 18

white vegetable fat,
   for greasing
175 g/6 oz self-raising flour
1 tsp baking powder
40 g/1$\frac{1}{2}$ oz caster sugar
1 medium egg
200 ml/7 fl oz milk
butter and syrup, to serve

Marbled Toffee Shortbread

1 Preheat the oven to 180°C/350°F/Gas Mark 4, 10 minutes before baking. Oil and line a 20.5 cm/8 inch square cake tin with nonstick baking parchment. Cream the butter and sugar until light and fluffy, then sift in the flour and cocoa powder. Add the semolina and mix together to form a soft dough. Press into the base of the prepared tin. Prick all over with a fork, then bake in the preheated oven for 25 minutes. Leave to cool.

2 To make the toffee filling, gently heat the butter, sugar and condensed milk together until the sugar has dissolved. Bring to the boil, then simmer for 5 minutes, stirring constantly. Leave for 1 minute, then spread over the shortbread and leave to cool.

3 For the topping, place the different chocolates in separate heatproof bowls and melt one at a time, set over a saucepan of almost-boiling water. Drop spoonfuls of each on top of the toffee and tilt the tin to cover evenly. Swirl with a knife for a marbled effect.

4 Leave the chocolate to cool. When just set, mark into fingers using a sharp knife. Leave for at least 1 hour to harden before cutting into fingers.

Ingredients   MAKES 12

175 g/6 oz butter
75 g/3 oz caster sugar
175 g/6 oz plain flour
25 g/1 oz cocoa powder
75 g/3 oz fine semolina

For the toffee filling:
50 g/2 oz butter
50 g/2 oz soft light brown sugar
397 g can condensed milk

For the chocolate topping:
75 g/3 oz plain dark chocolate
75 g/3 oz milk chocolate
75 g/3 oz white chocolate

Lemon & Ginger Buns

1 Preheat the oven to 220°C/425°F/Gas Mark 7, 15 minutes before baking. Cut the butter or margarine into small pieces and place in a large bowl.

2 Sift the flour, baking powder, ginger and salt together and add to the butter with the lemon zest. Using the fingertips, rub the butter into the flour and spice mixture until it resembles coarse breadcrumbs.

3 Stir in the sugar, sultanas, chopped mixed peel and stem ginger.

4 Add the egg and lemon juice to the mixture, then, using a round-bladed knife, stir well to mix. (The mixture should be quite stiff and just holding together.)

5 Place heaped tablespoons of the mixture on to a lightly oiled baking tray, making sure that the dollops of mixture are well apart.

6 Using a fork, rough up the edges of the buns and bake in the preheated oven for 12–15 minutes.

7 Leave the buns to cool for 5 minutes before transferring to a wire rack to cool, then serve. Otherwise, store the buns in an airtight container and eat within 3–5 days.

Ingredients   MAKES 15

175 g/6 oz butter or margarine
350 g/12 oz plain flour
2 tsp baking powder
$^1/_2$ tsp ground ginger
pinch salt
finely grated zest of 1 lemon
175 g/6 oz soft light brown sugar
125 g/4 oz sultanas
75 g/3 oz chopped mixed peel
25 g/1 oz stem ginger,
    finely chopped
1 medium egg
juice of 1 lemon

Tasty Tip

For a gooey, sticky treat, brush the buns with a little syrup from the jar of stem ginger and scatter with some extra finely chopped stem ginger, as soon as they have been removed from the oven.

2

4

6

Lemon Butter Biscuits

1 Preheat the oven to 170°C/325°F/Gas Mark 3. Grease two baking sheets. Place the butter into a bowl and beat together with the sugar until light and fluffy.

2 Sift in the flour and cornflour, add the lemon zest and mix together with a flat-bladed knife to form a soft dough.

3 Place the dough on a lightly floured surface, knead lightly and roll out thinly. Use biscuit cutters to cut out fancy shapes, re-rolling the trimmings to make more biscuits. Carefully lift each biscuit onto a baking sheet with a palette knife, then prick lightly with a fork.

4 Bake for 12–15 minutes. Cool on the baking sheets for 5 minutes, then place on a wire rack. Once completely cool, dust with caster sugar.

Ingredients   MAKES 14–18

175 g/6 oz butter, softened
75 g/3 oz caster sugar
175 g/6 oz plain flour
75 g/3 oz cornflour
zest of 1 lemon, finely grated
2 tbsp caster sugar, to decorate

Cantuccini

1 Preheat the oven to 180°C/350°F/Gas Mark 4. Line a large
   baking sheet with nonstick baking parchment. Place the flour,
   caster sugar, baking powder, vanilla extract, the whole eggs
   and one of the egg yolks into a food processor and blend
   until the mixture forms a ball, scraping down the sides once
   or twice. Turn the mixture out on to a lightly floured surface
   and knead in the chopped nuts and aniseed.

2 Divide the paste into three pieces and roll into logs about 4
   cm/1½ inches wide. Place the logs on to the baking sheet at
   least 5 cm/2 inches apart. Brush lightly with the other egg yolk
   beaten with 1 tablespoon of water and bake in the preheated
   oven for 30–35 minutes.

3 Remove from the oven and reduce the oven temperature
   to 150°C/300°F/Gas Mark 2. Cut the logs diagonally into
   2.5 cm/1 inch slices and lay cut-side down on the baking
   sheet. Return to the oven for a further 30–40 minutes until
   dry and firm. Cool on a wire rack and store in an airtight
   container. Serve with Vin Santo or coffee.

Ingredients   MAKES 24

250 g/9 oz plain flour
250 g/9 oz caster sugar
½ tsp baking powder
½ tsp vanilla extract
2 medium eggs
1 medium egg yolk
100 g/3½ oz mixed almonds and
   hazelnuts, toasted and roughly
   chopped
1 tsp whole aniseed
1 medium egg yolk mixed with
   1 tbsp water, to glaze
Vin Santo or coffee, to serve

Food Fact

Cantuccini are simply small biscuits,
traditionally served with a sweet
dessert wine called Vin Santo.
Cantucci are large biscuits that are
made in the same way.

1

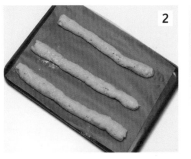

2

2

Puddings & Decadent Desserts

Don't forget about all the other wonderful sweet concoctions that can be baked in your oven: sponge puddings, bread puddings, rice puddings, meringues, crumbles... Here choose from the traditional, such as Rice Pudding, Summer Pavlova and Bread & Butter Pudding, or go for the more indulgent and different, such as Chocolate Brioche Bake, Hazelnut Meringues with Chocolate Sauce or Baked Stuffed Amaretti Peaches.

Oaty Fruit Puddings

1 Preheat the oven to 200°C/400°F/Gas Mark 6. Lightly oil and line the bases of four individual pudding bowls or muffin tins with a small circle of greaseproof paper.

2 Mix together the oats, butter, nuts, honey and cinnamon in a small bowl.

3 Using a spoon, spread two thirds of the oaty mixture over the base and around the sides of the pudding bowls or muffin tins.

4 Toss together the pears and marmalade and spoon into the oaty cases.

5 Scatter over the remaining oaty mixture to cover the pears and marmalade.

6 Bake in the preheated oven for 15–20 minutes until cooked and the tops of the puddings are golden and crisp.

7 Leave for 5 minutes before removing the pudding bowls or the muffin tins. Decorate with orange zest and serve hot with custard or fruit-flavoured yogurt.

Ingredients SERVES 4

125 g/4 oz rolled oats
50 g/2 oz butter, melted
2 tbsp chopped almonds
1 tbsp clear honey
pinch of ground cinnamon
2 pears, peeled, cored and finely chopped
1 tbsp marmalade
orange zest, to decorate
custard or fruit-flavoured yogurt, to serve

Tasty Tip

Liqueur custard is superb with steamed and baked puddings. Add 2–3 tablespoons of either Cointreau or a liqueur of your choice to the custard, together with 1 teaspoon of vanilla extract. Taste the custard and add more alcohol if desired.

Rice Pudding

1   Preheat the oven to 150°C/300°F/Gas Mark 2. Lightly oil a large ovenproof dish.

2   Sprinkle the rice and the sugar into the dish and mix.

3   Bring the evaporated milk and milk to the boil in a small pan, stirring occasionally.

4   Stir the milks into the rice and mix well until the rice is coated thoroughly.

5   Sprinkle over the nutmeg, cover with foil and bake in the preheated oven for 30 minutes.

6   Remove the pudding from the oven and stir well, breaking up any lumps.

7   Cover with the same foil. Bake in the oven for a further 30 minutes. Remove from the oven and stir well again.

8   Dot the pudding with butter and bake for a further 45–60 minutes until the rice is tender and the skin is browned.

9   Divide the pudding into four individual serving bowls. Top with a large spoonful of the jam and serve immediately.

Ingredients   SERVES 4

65 g/2^1/$_2$ oz pudding rice
50 g/2 oz granulated sugar
410 g can light evaporated milk
300 ml/^{1}/$_2$ pint semi-skimmed milk
pinch of freshly grated nutmeg
25 g/1 oz butter
jam, to decorate

Tasty Tip

Traditionally, rice pudding was cooked alongside the Sunday roast and, after many hours in the oven, came out rich and creamy. The main trick to achieving traditional creamy rice pudding is not using cream and full-fat milk, but instead long, slow cooking at a low temperature. Try adding a few sultanas and lemon peel or a few roughly crushed cardamom pods for an alternative flavour. It is also delicious dusted with a little ground cinnamon.

Chocolate Brioche Bake

1. Preheat the oven to 180°C/350°F/Gas Mark 4, 10 minutes before baking. Lightly oil or butter a 1.7 litre/3 pint ovenproof dish. Melt the chocolate with 25 g/1 oz of the butter in a heatproof bowl set over a saucepan of simmering water. Stir until smooth.

2. Arrange half of the sliced brioche in the ovenproof dish, overlapping the slices slightly, then pour over half of the melted chocolate. Repeat the layers, finishing with a layer of chocolate.

3. Melt the remaining butter in a saucepan. Remove from the heat and stir in the orange oil or zest, the nutmeg and the beaten eggs. Continuing to stir, add the sugar and finally the milk. Beat thoroughly and pour over the brioche. Leave to stand for 30 minutes before baking.

4. Bake on the centre shelf in the preheated oven for 45 minutes, or until the custard is set and the topping is golden brown. Leave to stand for 5 minutes, then dust with cocoa powder and icing sugar. Serve warm.

Ingredients
SERVES 6

200 g/7 oz plain dark chocolate, broken into pieces
75 g/3 oz unsalted butter
225 g/8 oz brioche, sliced
1 tsp pure orange oil or 1 tbsp grated orange zest
$1/2$ tsp freshly grated nutmeg
3 medium eggs, beaten
25 g/1 oz golden caster sugar
600 ml/1 pint milk
cocoa powder and icing sugar, for dusting

Helpful Hint
Croissants, fruit buns or fruit loaves are also suitable for this recipe. It is important that the dish is left to stand for 30 minutes before baking – do not be tempted to omit this step.

Chocolate Pear Pudding

1 Preheat the oven to 190°C/375°F/Gas Mark 5, 10 minutes before baking. Butter a 20.5 cm/8 inch sandwich tin with 15 g/½ oz of the butter and sprinkle the base with the soft brown sugar. Arrange the drained pear halves on top of the sugar, cut-side down. Fill the spaces between the pears with the walnut halves, flat-side upwards.

2 Cream the remaining butter with the caster sugar, then gradually beat in the beaten eggs, adding 1 tablespoon of the flour after each addition. When all the eggs have been added, stir in the remaining flour.

3 Sift the cocoa powder and baking powder together, then stir into the creamed mixture with 1–2 tablespoons of the reserved pear juice to give a smooth dropping consistency.

4 Spoon the mixture over the pear halves, smoothing the surface. Bake in the preheated oven for 20–25 minutes until well risen and the surface springs back when lightly pressed.

5 Remove from the oven and leave to cool for 5 minutes. Using a palette knife, loosen the sides and invert onto a serving plate. Serve with custard.

Ingredients   SERVES 6

130 g/4½ oz butter, softened
2 tbsp soft brown sugar
400 g can pear halves, drained and
    juice reserved
25 g/1 oz walnut halves
125 g/4 oz golden caster sugar
2 medium eggs, beaten
75 g/3 oz self-raising flour, sifted
50 g/2 oz cocoa powder
1 tsp baking powder
prepared chocolate custard,
    to serve

Tasty Tip
You could substitute fresh pears for the tinned ones in this recipe. However, they would need to be poached first in a light syrup, otherwise they would discolour in the oven.

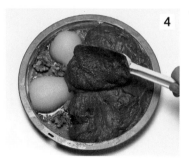

Peach & Chocolate Bake

1 Preheat the oven to 170°C/325°F/Gas Mark 3, 10 minutes before baking. Lightly oil a 1.7 litre/3 pint ovenproof dish.

2 Break the chocolate and butter into small pieces and place in a small heatproof bowl set over a saucepan of gently simmering water. Ensure the water is not touching the base of the bowl, and leave to melt. Remove the bowl from the heat and stir until smooth.

3 Whisk the egg yolks with the sugar until very thick and creamy, then stir the melted chocolate and butter into the whisked egg yolk mixture and mix together lightly.

4 Place the egg whites in a clean grease-free bowl and whisk until stiff, then fold 2 tablespoons of the whisked egg whites into the chocolate mixture. Mix well, then add the remaining egg white and fold in very lightly.

5 Fold the peach slices and the cinnamon into the mixture, then spoon the mixture into the prepared dish. Do not level the mixture, leave a little uneven.

6 Bake in the preheated oven for 35–40 minutes until well risen and just firm to the touch. Sprinkle the bake with the icing sugar and serve immediately with spoonfuls of crème fraîche.

Ingredients   SERVES 6

200 g/7 oz plain dark chocolate
125 g/4 oz unsalted butter
4 medium eggs, separated
125 g/4 oz caster sugar
425 g can peach slices, drained
$^1/_2$ tsp ground cinnamon
1 tbsp icing sugar, sifted, to decorate
crème fraîche, to serve

Helpful Hint

As this cake contains no flour, it has a very light texture. It is very important to fold the ingredients together very lightly, otherwise the air will be knocked out of the mixture.

Sticky Chocolate Surprise Pudding

1   Preheat the oven to 180°C/350°F/Gas Mark 4, 10 minutes before baking. Lightly oil a 1.5 litre/2½ pint ovenproof soufflé dish. Sift the flour and cocoa powder into a large bowl and stir in the caster sugar and the chopped mint-flavoured chocolate and make a well in the centre.

2   Whisk the milk, vanilla extract and the melted butter together, then beat in the egg. Pour into the well in the dry ingredients and gradually mix together, drawing the dry ingredients in from the sides of the bowl. Beat well until thoroughly mixed. Spoon into the prepared soufflé dish.

3   To make the sauce, blend the dark muscovado sugar and the cocoa powder together and mix with the hot water until the sugar and cocoa have dissolved. Carefully pour over the top of the pudding, but do not stir in.

4   Bake in the preheated oven for 35–40 minutes until firm to the touch and the mixture has formed a sauce underneath. Decorate with mint and serve immediately.

Ingredients   SERVES 6–8

150 g/5 oz self-raising flour
25 g/1 oz cocoa powder
200 g/7 oz golden caster sugar
75 g/3 oz mint-flavoured chocolate, chopped
175 ml/6 fl oz full-cream milk
2 tsp vanilla extract
50 g/2 oz unsalted butter, melted
1 medium egg
fresh mint sprigs, to decorate

For the sauce:

175 g/6 oz dark muscovado sugar
125 g/4 oz cocoa powder
600 ml/1 pint very hot water

Food Fact

The surprise is that this pudding separates during cooking to give a sticky chocolate cake with a chocolate custard sauce underneath.

1

2

3

Chocolate Pancakes

1 Preheat the oven to 200°C/400°F/Gas Mark 6, 15 minutes before baking. To make the pancakes, sift the flour, cocoa powder, sugar and nutmeg into a bowl and make a well in the centre. Beat the eggs and milk together, then gradually beat into the flour mixture to form a batter. Stir in 50 g/2 oz of the melted butter and leave to stand for 1 hour. Heat an 18 cm/7 inch nonstick frying pan and brush with a little melted butter. Add about 3 tablespoons of the batter and swirl to cover the base of the pan. Cook over a medium heat for 1–2 minutes, flip over and cook for a further 40 seconds. Repeat with the remaining batter. Stack the pancakes between greaseproof paper.

2 To make the sauce, place the mango, white wine and sugar in a saucepan and bring to the boil over a medium heat, then simmer for 2–3 minutes, stirring constantly. When the mixture has thickened, add the rum. Chill in the refrigerator.

3 For the filling, melt the chocolate and cream in a heavy-based saucepan over a medium heat. Stir until smooth, then leave to cool. Beat the yolks with the caster sugar for 3–5 minutes until the mixture is pale and creamy, then beat in the chocolate mixture. Beat the egg whites until stiff, then add a little to the chocolate mixture. Stir in the remainder. Spoon a little of the mixture onto a pancake. Fold in half, then half again, forming a triangle. Repeat with the remaining pancakes, brush with a little melted butter and bake in the oven for 15–20 minutes until the filling is set. Serve hot or cold with the mango sauce.

Ingredients   SERVES 6

For the pancakes:
75 g/3 oz plain flour
1 tbsp cocoa powder
1 tsp caster sugar
$1/_2$ tsp freshly grated nutmeg
2 medium eggs
175 ml/6 fl oz milk
75 g/3 oz unsalted butter, melted

For the mango sauce:
1 ripe mango, peeled and diced
50 ml/2 fl oz white wine
2 tbsp golden caster sugar
2 tbsp rum

For the filling:
225 g/8 oz plain dark chocolate
85 ml/3 fl oz double cream
3 eggs, separated
25 g/1 oz golden caster sugar

1

1

3

Chocolate Meringue Nests with Fruity Filling

1   Preheat the oven to 110°C/225°F/Gas Mark ¹/₄, 5 minutes before baking and line a baking sheet with nonstick baking parchment. Place the hazelnuts and 2 tablespoons of the caster sugar in a food processor and blend to a powder. Add the chocolate and blend again until the chocolate is roughly chopped.

2   In a clean, grease-free bowl, whisk the egg whites and salt until soft peaks form. Gradually whisk in the remaining sugar a teaspoonful at a time and continue to whisk until the meringue is stiff and shiny. Fold in the cornflour and the white wine vinegar with the chocolate and hazelnut mixture.

3   Spoon the mixture into eight mounds, about 10 cm/4 inches in diameter, on the baking parchment. Do not worry if not perfect shapes. Make a hollow in each mound, then place in the preheated oven. Cook for 1¹/₂ hours, then switch the oven off and leave in the oven until cool.

4   To make the filling, whip the cream until soft peaks form. In another bowl, beat the mascarpone cheese until it is softened, then mix with the cream. Spoon the mixture into the meringue nests and top with the fresh fruits. Decorate with a few chocolate curls and serve.

Ingredients   SERVES 8

125 g/4 oz hazelnuts, toasted
125 g/4 oz golden caster sugar
75 g/3 oz plain dark chocolate,
    broken into pieces
2 medium egg whites
pinch salt
1 tsp cornflour
¹/₂ tsp white wine vinegar
chocolate curls, to decorate

For the filling:

150 ml/¹/₄ pint double cream
150 g/5 oz mascarpone cheese
prepared summer fruits, such as
    strawberries, raspberries and
    redcurrants

Chocolate Rice Pudding Brûlée

1 Preheat the oven to 150°C/300°F/Gas Mark 2, 10 minutes before cooking. Preheat the grill on high when ready to use. Gradually blend the cocoa powder with 3 tablespoons boiling water to form a soft smooth paste. Place the rice and milk, bay leaf, orange zest and the cocoa powder paste in a saucepan. Bring to the boil, stirring constantly.

2 Reduce the heat and simmer for 20 minutes, or until the rice is tender. Remove from the heat and discard the bay leaf, then add the white chocolate and stir until melted.

3 Whisk together the caster sugar and egg yolks until thick, then stir in the cream. Stir in the rice mixture together with the vanilla extract. Pour into a buttered shallow dish. Stand the dish in a baking tin with sufficient hot water to come halfway up the sides of the dish. Cook in the preheated oven for 1½ hours, or until set. Stir occasionally during cooking, either removing the skin from the top or stirring the skin into the pudding. Remove from the tin and leave until cool.

4 When ready to serve, sprinkle the demerara sugar over the surface of the rice pudding. Place under the preheated grill and cook until the sugar melts and caramelises, turning the dish occasionally. Either serve immediately or chill in the refrigerator for 1 hour before serving.

Ingredients SERVES 6

2 tbsp cocoa powder
75 g/3 oz short-grain rice
600 ml/1 pint milk
1 bay leaf
grated zest of 1 orange
50 g/2 oz white chocolate,
    roughly chopped
1 tbsp golden caster sugar
4 medium egg yolks
225 ml/8 fl oz double cream
½ tsp vanilla extract
4 tbsp demerara sugar

Tasty Tip

Short-grain rice is often labelled 'pudding rice'. The rice is short, quite fat and pearly in appearance. It has a great deal of starch, which comes out of the rice during the long cooking and helps to make the finished dish very creamy.

Eve's Pudding

1 Preheat the oven to 180°C/350°F/Gas Mark 4. Oil a 1.1 litre/
2 pint baking dish. Peel, core and slice the apples and place a
layer in the base of the prepared dish.

2 Sprinkle over some of the blackberries, a little demerara sugar
and lemon zest. Continue to layer the apple and blackberries in
this way until all the ingredients have been used.

3 Cream the sugar and butter together until light and fluffy. Beat
in the vanilla extract and then the eggs a little at a time, adding
a spoonful of flour after each addition. Fold in the extra flour
with a metal spoon or rubber spatula and mix well.

4 Spread the sponge mixture over the top of the fruit and level
with the back of a spoon. Place the dish on a baking sheet and
bake in the preheated oven for 35–40 minutes until well risen
and golden brown. (To test if the pudding is cooked, press the
cooked sponge lightly with a clean finger – if it springs back, the
sponge is cooked.) Dust the pudding with a little icing sugar and
serve immediately with the custard.

Ingredients   SERVES 6

450 g/1 lb cooking apples
175 g/6 oz blackberries
75 g/3 oz demerara sugar
grated zest of 1 lemon
125 g/4 oz caster sugar
125 g/4 oz butter
few drops vanilla extract
2 medium eggs, beaten
125 g/4 oz self-raising flour
1 tbsp icing sugar
ready-made custard, to serve

Food Fact

Eve's Pudding is a classic English
pudding and has been popular since
the early 20th century. At that time,
there were many different varieties of
cooking apples grown throughout the
country. Unfortunately, many of
these apples have now disappeared.

College Pudding

1 Preheat the oven to 180˚C/350˚F/Gas Mark 4. Lightly oil an ovenproof 900 ml/1¹/₂ pint ovenproof pudding basin and place a small circle of greaseproof paper in the base.

2 Mix the shredded suet and breadcrumbs together and rub lightly together with the fingertips to remove any lumps.

3 Stir in the dried fruit, spices, sugar and baking powder. Add the eggs and beat lightly together until the mixture is well blended and the fruit is evenly distributed.

4 Spoon the mixture into the prepared pudding basin and level the surface. Place on a baking tray and cover lightly with some greaseproof paper.

5 Bake in the preheated oven for 20 minutes, then remove the paper and continue to bake for a further 10–15 minutes until the top is firm.

6 When the pudding is cooked, remove from the oven and carefully turn out on to a warmed serving dish. Decorate with the orange zest and serve immediately.

Ingredients   SERVES 4

125 g/4 oz shredded suet
125 g/4 oz fresh white breadcrumbs
50 g/2 oz sultanas
50 g/2 oz seedless raisins
¹/₂ tsp ground cinnamon
¹/₄ tsp freshly grated nutmeg
¹/₄ tsp mixed spice
50 g/2 oz caster sugar
¹/₂ tsp baking powder
2 medium eggs, beaten
orange zest, to garnish

Tasty Tip

Like many other suet puddings this recipe is relatively cheap to make. For extra fruitiness, add some apple purée to the mixture. To make it, peel, core and chop 1 cooking apple. Place in a saucepan with 25 g/1 oz sugar and 4 tablespoons water. Simmer until softened but not falling apart, then roughly mash. Add the purée to the mixture in step 3 and continue as before.

Osborne Pudding

1 Preheat the oven to 170°C/325°F/Gas Mark 3. Lightly oil a 1.1 litre/2 pint baking dish. Remove the crusts from the bread and spread thickly with butter and marmalade. Cut the bread into small triangles. Place half the bread in the base of the dish and sprinkle over the dried mixed fruit, 1 tablespoon of the orange juice and half the caster sugar. Top with the remaining bread and marmalade, buttered side up, and pour over the remaining orange juice. Sprinkle over the remaining caster sugar.

2 Whisk the eggs with the milk and cream and pour over the pudding. Reserve for about 30 minutes to allow the bread to absorb the liquid.

3 Place in a roasting tin and pour in enough boiling water to come halfway up the sides of the dish. Bake in the preheated oven for 50–60 minutes until the pudding is set and the top is crisp and golden.

4 Meanwhile, make the marmalade sauce. Heat the orange zest and juice with the marmalade and brandy if using. Mix 1 tablespoon water with the cornflour and mix together well. Add to the saucepan and cook on a low heat, stirring, until warmed through and thickened. Serve the pudding hot with the marmalade sauce.

Ingredients   SERVES 4

8 slices white bread
50 g/2 oz butter
2 tbsp marmalade
50 g/2 oz luxury mixed dried fruit
2 tbsp fresh orange juice
40 g/1½ oz caster sugar
2 large eggs
450 ml/¾ pint milk
150 ml/¼ pint whipping cream

For the marmalade sauce:

zest and juice of 1 orange
2 tbsp thick-cut orange marmalade
1 tbsp brandy (optional)
2 tsp cornflour

Tasty Tip

To make an orange sauce instead, omit the marmalade and add the juice of another 3 oranges and a squeeze of lemon juice to make 250 ml/8 fl oz. Follow the recipe as before but increase the cornflour to 1½ tablespoons.

Hazelnut Meringues with Chocolate Sauce

1 Preheat the oven to 150°C/300°F/Gas Mark 2, 10 minutes before baking. Line two baking sheets with nonstick baking parchment. Whisk the egg whites in a large grease–free bowl until stiff, then add the caster sugar, 1 teaspoonful at a time, whisking well after each addition. Continue to whisk until the mixture is stiff and dry, then, using a metal spoon, fold in the ground hazelnuts.

2 Using two dessertspoons, spoon the mixture into 12 quenelle shapes onto the baking parchment. Sprinkle over the toasted hazelnuts and bake in the preheated oven for 1^1/$_2$–2 hours until dry and crisp. Switch the oven off and leave to cool in the oven.

3 To make the chocolate sauce, place the chocolate with the butter and 4 tablespoons of the cream and the golden syrup in a heavy–based saucepan and heat, stirring occasionally, until the chocolate has melted and the mixture is blended. Do not boil. Whip the remaining cream until soft peaks form.

4 Sandwich the meringues together with the whipped cream and place on serving plates. Spoon over the sauce and serve with a few fresh berries.

Ingredients   SERVES 6

4 medium egg whites
225 g/8 oz caster sugar
125 g/4 oz ground hazelnuts
50 g/2 oz toasted hazelnuts, sliced
fresh berries, such as raspberries,
    strawberries and blueberries,
    to serve

For the chocolate sauce:
225 g/8 oz plain dark chocolate,
    broken into pieces
50 g/2 oz butter
300 ml/^{1}/$_2$ pint double cream
1 tbsp golden syrup

Helpful Hint
It is important to add the sugar gradually when making meringues because if the sugar is not fully dissolved into the egg white it might leach out during cooking, making the meringues 'sweat'.

Chocolate Rice Pudding

1   Preheat the oven to 170°C/325°F/Gas Mark 3, 10 minutes before cooking. Lightly butter a large ovenproof dish. Rinse the pudding rice, then place in the base of the buttered dish and sprinkle over the caster sugar.

2   Pour the evaporated milk and milk into a heavy-based saucepan and bring slowly to the boil over a low heat, stirring occasionally to avoid sticking. Pour the milk over the rice and sugar and stir well until well mixed and the sugar has dissolved.

3   Grate a little nutmeg over the top, then sprinkle with the ground cinnamon, if liked. Cover tightly with foil and bake in the preheated oven for 30 minutes.

4   Remove the pudding from the oven and stir well to break up any lumps that may have formed. Cover with foil and return to the oven for a further 30 minutes. Remove the pudding from the oven once again and stir to break up any more lumps.

5   Stir the chocolate chips into the rice pudding and then dot with the butter. Continue to bake, uncovered, in the oven for a further 45 minutes–1 hour until the rice is tender and the skin is golden brown. Serve warm, with or without the skin, according to personal preference. Serve with a few sliced strawberries and a spoonful of crème fraîche.

Ingredients   SERVES 4

65 g/2½ oz pudding rice
75 g/3 oz caster sugar
1 x 410 g can evaporated milk
600 ml/1 pint milk
pinch freshly grated nutmeg
¼ tsp ground cinnamon (optional)
50 g/2 oz plain chocolate chips
25 g/1 oz butter
freshly sliced strawberries, to
    decorate
crème fraîche, to serve

Tasty Tip

If chocolate chips are unavailable, use a piece of plain chocolate and chop it into small pieces instead.

Topsy Turvy Pudding

1 Preheat the oven to 180°C/350°F/Gas Mark 4, 10 minutes before baking. Lightly oil a 20.5 cm/8 inch deep round loose-bottomed cake tin. Place the demerara sugar and 3 tablespoons water in a small heavy-based saucepan and heat gently until the sugar has dissolved. Swirl the saucepan or stir with a clean wooden spoon to ensure the sugar has dissolved, then bring to the boil and boil rapidly until a golden caramel is formed. Pour into the bottom of the tin and leave to cool.

2 For the sponge, cream the butter and sugar together until light and fluffy. Gradually beat in the eggs a little at a time, beating well after each addition. Add a spoonful of flour after each addition to prevent the mixture curdling. Add the melted chocolate and then stir well. Fold in the orange zest, self-raising flour and sifted cocoa powder and mix well.

3 Remove the peel from both oranges, taking care to remove as much of the pith as possible. Thinly slice the peel into strips and then slice the oranges. Arrange the peel and then the orange slices over the caramel. Top with the sponge mixture and level the top. Place the tin on a baking sheet and bake in the preheated oven for 40–45 minutes until well risen, golden brown and an inserted skewer comes out clean. Remove from the oven, leave for about 5 minutes, invert onto a serving plate and sprinkle with cocoa powder. Serve with either custard or sour cream.

Ingredients   SERVES 6

For the topping:
175 g/6 oz demerara sugar
2 oranges

For the sponge:
175 g/6 oz butter, softened
175 g/6 oz caster sugar
3 medium eggs, beaten
175 g/6 oz self-raising flour, sifted
50 g/2 oz plain dark chocolate,
    melted
grated zest of 1 orange
25 g/1 oz cocoa powder, sifted
custard or sour cream, to serve

Helpful Hint

When making the caramel in step 1, make sure the sugar has completely dissolved and that no sugar remains clinging to the side of the pan, otherwise the caramel will crystallise.

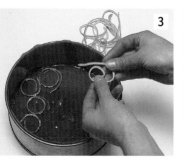

Bread & Butter Pudding

1 Preheat the oven to 180°C/350°F/Gas Mark 4, 10 minutes before cooking. Lightly butter a 1.1 litre/2 pint ovenproof dish.

2 Butter the bread and cut into quarters. Arrange half the bread in the dish and scatter over two thirds of the dried fruit and sugar. Repeat the layering, finishing with the dried fruits.

3 Beat the eggs and milk together and pour over the bread and butter. Leave to stand for 30 minutes.

4 Sprinkle with the remaining sugar and a little nutmeg and carefully place in the oven. Cook for 40 minutes, or until the pudding has lightly set and the top is golden.

5 Remove and sprinkle with a little extra sugar, if liked. Serve with freshly made custard.

Ingredients   SERVES 4–6

2–3 tbsp unsalted butter, softened
4–6 slices white bread
75 g/3 oz mixed dried fruits
25 g/1 oz caster sugar, plus
    extra for sprinkling
2 medium eggs
450 ml/$^3/_4$ pint semi-skimmed
    milk, warmed
freshly grated nutmeg
freshly made custard, to serve

Fruity Chocolate Bread Pudding

1 Preheat the oven to 180°C/350°F/Gas Mark 4, 10 minutes before cooking. Lightly butter a shallow ovenproof dish. Break the chocolate into small pieces, then place in a heatproof bowl set over a saucepan of gently simmering water. Heat gently, stirring frequently, until the chocolate has melted and is smooth. Remove from the heat and leave for about 10 minutes until the chocolate begins to thicken slightly.

2 Cut the fruit loaf into medium to thick slices, then spread with the melted chocolate. Leave until almost set, then cut each slice in half to form a triangle. Layer the chocolate-coated bread slices and the chopped apricots in the buttered ovenproof dish.

3 Stir the cream and the milk together, then stir in the caster sugar. Beat the eggs, then gradually beat in the cream and milk mixture. Beat thoroughly until well blended. Carefully pour over the bread slices and apricots and leave to stand for 30 minutes.

4 Sprinkle with the demerara sugar and place in a roasting tin half filled with boiling water. Cook in the preheated oven for 45 minutes, or until golden and the custard is lightly set. Serve immediately.

Ingredients   SERVES 4

175 g/6 oz plain dark chocolate
1 small fruit loaf
125 g/4 oz ready-to-eat dried
    apricots, roughly chopped
450 ml/³/₄ pint single cream
300 ml/¹/₂ pint milk
1 tbsp caster sugar
3 medium eggs
3 tbsp demerara sugar,
    for sprinkling

Helpful Hint

It is important to leave the pudding to stand for at least 30 minutes, as described in step 3. This allows the custard to soak into the bread – otherwise it sets around the bread as it cooks, making the pudding seem stodgy.

Chocolate & Fruit Crumble

1 Preheat the oven to 190°C/375°F/Gas Mark 5, 10 minutes before baking. Lightly oil an ovenproof dish.

2 For the crumble, sift the flour into a large bowl. Cut the butter into small dice and add to the flour. Rub the butter into the flour until the mixture resembles fine breadcrumbs.

3 Stir the sugar, porridge oats and the chopped hazelnuts into the mixture and reserve.

4 For the filling, peel the apples, then core and slice thickly. Place in a large heavy-based saucepan with the lemon juice and 3 tablespoons water. Add the sultanas, raisins and the soft brown sugar. Bring slowly to the boil, cover and simmer over a gentle heat for 8–10 minutes, stirring occasionally until the apples are slightly softened.

5 Remove the saucepan from the heat and leave to cool slightly before stirring in the pears, ground cinnamon and the chopped chocolate.

6 Spoon into the prepared ovenproof dish. Sprinkle the crumble evenly over the top, then bake in the preheated oven for 35–40 minutes until the top is golden. Remove from the oven, sprinkle with the caster sugar and serve immediately.

Ingredients   SERVES 4

For the crumble:
125 g/4 oz plain flour
125 g/4 oz butter
75 g/3 oz light soft brown sugar
50 g/2 oz rolled porridge oats
50 g/2 oz hazelnuts, chopped

For the filling:
450 g/1 lb bramley apples
1 tbsp lemon juice
50 g/2 oz sultanas
50 g/2 oz seedless raisins
50 g/2 oz light soft brown sugar
350 g/12 oz pears, peeled, cored
   and chopped
1 tsp ground cinnamon
125 g/4 oz plain dark chocolate, very
   roughly chopped
2 tsp caster sugar, for sprinkling

Chocolate Hazelnut Meringue Gateau

1 Preheat the oven to 150°C/300°F/Gas Mark 2, 5 minutes before baking. Cut three pieces of baking parchment into 30.5 cm x 12.5 cm/12 inch x 5 inch rectangles and then place onto two or three baking sheets. Whisk the egg whites until stiff, add half the sugar and whisk until stiff, smooth and glossy. Whisk in the remaining sugar, 1 tablespoon at a time, beating well after each addition. When all the sugar has been added, whisk for 1 minute. Stir in the nuts. Spoon the meringue inside the rectangles, spreading in a continuous backwards and forwards movement. Bake in the oven for 1¹/₄ hours, remove and leave until cold. Trim the meringues until they measure 25.5 cm x 10 cm/10 inches x 4 inches. Reserve the trimmings.

2 Melt the chocolate and the butter in a heatproof bowl set over a saucepan of gently simmering water and stir until smooth. Remove from the heat and beat in the yolks. Whisk the egg whites until stiff, then whisk in the icing sugar a little at a time. Fold the whites into the chocolate mixture and chill for 20–30 minutes until thick enough to spread. Whip the double cream until soft peaks form. Reserve. Place one of the meringue layers onto a serving plate. Spread with about half of the mousse mixture, then top with a second meringue layer. Spread the remaining mousse mixture over the top with the third meringue. Spread the cream over the top and sprinkle with the chopped hazelnuts. Chill in the refrigerator for at least 4 hours and up to 24 hours. Serve cut into slices.

Ingredients   8–10 SLICES

5 medium egg whites
275 g/10 oz caster sugar
125 g/4 oz hazelnuts, toasted and
    finely chopped
175 g/6 oz plain dark chocolate
100 g/3¹/₂ oz butter
3 medium eggs, separated, plus
    1 medium egg white
25 g/1 oz icing sugar
125 ml/4 fl oz double cream
hazelnuts, toasted and chopped,
    to decorate

Tasty Tip
This cake can be round. Make the meringues into circles measuring 20.5 cm/8 inches. Trim to 18 cm/ 7 inches before assembling.

1

2

2

Chocolate Melting Pots

1 Preheat the oven to 160°C/325°F/Gas Mark 3, 10 minutes before cooking. Lightly butter four individual pudding basins or four 150 ml/¼ pint ramekins, then dust the inside of each with a little of the cocoa powder, by tipping some cocoa powder into the bottom and then turning and tapping the side of the dish until the inside is coated.

2 Break the chocolate into small pieces and place in a heatproof bowl set over a pan of gently simmering water. Leave until softened, then remove from the heat. Add the remaining butter and stir until smooth. Reserve.

3 Place a large mixing bowl over a pan of gently simmering water and add the eggs, egg yolks and sugar. Whisk until thick and creamy. Remove from the heat, stir in the melted chocolate and leave to cool for 5 minutes.

4 Sift the flour over the mixture and gently fold in together with the ground almonds using a figure-of-eight movement. Spoon into the prepared pudding basins or ramekins, filling them three-quarters full.

5 Place on a baking sheet and cook for 12 minutes, or until the tops feel firm. Remove from the oven and invert onto serving plates. Dust with a little icing sugar, if using, and serve with raspberries and whipped cream.

Ingredients SERVES 4

125 g/4 oz unsalted butter, plus
  1 tsp for buttering
1 tbsp cocoa powder
125 g/4 oz good-quality
  dark chocolate
2 medium eggs
2 medium egg yolks
150 g/5 oz caster sugar
150 g/5 oz plain flour
1 tbsp ground almonds
icing sugar, for dusting (optional)
fresh raspberries and whipped cream,
  to serve

Lemon Surprise

1 Preheat the oven to 190°C/375°F/Gas Mark 5. Lightly oil a deep ovenproof dish.

2 Beat together the margarine and sugar until pale and fluffy.

3 Add the egg yolks, one at a time, with 1 tablespoon of the flour and beat well after each addition. Once added, stir in the remaining flour.

4 Stir in the milk, 4 tablespoons of the lemon juice and 3 tablespoons of the orange juice.

5 Whisk the egg whites until stiff and fold into the pudding mixture with a metal spoon or rubber spatula until well combined. Pour into the prepared dish.

6 Stand the dish in a roasting tin and pour in just enough boiling water to come halfway up the sides of the dish.

7 Bake in the preheated oven for 45 minutes until well risen and spongy to the touch.

8 Remove the pudding from the oven and sprinkle with the icing sugar. Decorate with the lemon twists and serve immediately with the strawberries.

Ingredients   SERVES 4

75 g/3 oz margarine
175 g/6 oz caster sugar
3 medium eggs, separated
75 g/3 oz self-raising flour
450 ml/³/₄ pint milk
juice of 2 lemons
juice of 1 orange
2 tsp icing sugar
lemon twists, to decorate
sliced strawberries, to serve

Food Fact

This recipe uses a bain-marie (when the dish is placed in a tin as in step 6), which enables the pudding to cook more slowly. This is necessary, as margarine does not respond well if baked at high temperatures.

Hazelnut, Chocolate & Chestnut Meringue Torte

1 Preheat the oven to 130°C/250°F/Gas Mark ½. Line three baking sheets with baking parchment and draw a 20.5 cm/8 inch circle on each. Beat 1 egg white until stiff peaks form. Beat in 25 g/1 oz of the sugar until shiny. Mix the cocoa powder with the remaining 25 g/1 oz of sugar and add 1 tablespoon at a time, beating well after each addition, until all the sugar is added and the mixture is stiff and glossy. Spread on to one of the baking sheets within the circle on the underside. Put the hazelnuts in a food processor and blend until chopped. In a clean bowl, beat the 2 egg whites until stiff. Add 50 g/2 oz of the sugar and beat. Add the remaining sugar about 1 tablespoon at a time, beating after each addition until all the sugar is added and the mixture is stiff and glossy. Reserve 2 tablespoons of the nuts, then fold in the remainder and divide between the 2 remaining baking sheets. Sprinkle one of the hazelnut meringues with the reserved hazelnuts and transfer all the baking sheets to the oven. Bake for 1½ hours. Turn the oven off and leave there until cold.

2 Whip the cream until thick. Beat the purée in another bowl until soft. Fold in a spoonful of the cream, then add the remaining cream and melted chocolate and fold together. Place the plain hazelnut meringue on a serving plate. Top with half the cream and chestnut mixture. Add the chocolate meringue and top with the remaining cream. Add the final meringue. Sprinkle over the grated chocolate and serve.

Ingredients   SERVES 8–10

For the chocolate meringue:
1 medium egg white
50 g/2 oz caster sugar
2 tbsp cocoa powder

For the hazelnut meringue:
75 g/3 oz hazelnuts, toasted
2 medium egg whites
125 g/4 oz caster sugar

For the filling:
300 ml/½ pint double cream
250 g can sweetened chestnut purée
50 g/2 oz plain dark chocolate, melted
25 g/1 oz plain dark chocolate, grated

Fruity Roulade

1 Preheat the oven to 220°C/425°F/Gas Mark 7. Lightly oil and line a 33 x 23 cm/13 x 9 inch Swiss roll tin with greaseproof paper or baking parchment.

2 Using an electric whisk, whisk the eggs and sugar until the mixture is doubled in volume and leaves a trail across the top.

3 Fold in the flour with a metal spoon or rubber spatula. Pour into the prepared tin and bake in the preheated oven for 10–12 minutes until well risen and golden.

4 Place a whole sheet of greaseproof paper or baking parchment out on a flat work surface and sprinkle evenly with caster sugar.

5 Turn the cooked sponge out on to the paper, discard the lining paper on top, trim the sponge and roll up encasing the paper inside. Reserve until cool.

6 To make the filling, mix together the Quark, yogurt, caster sugar, liqueur (if using) and orange zest. Unroll the roulade and spread over the mixture. Scatter over the strawberries and roll up.

7 Decorate the roulade with the strawberries. Dust with the icing sugar and serve.

Ingredients   SERVES 4

For the sponge:
3 medium eggs
75 g/3 oz caster sugar
75 g/3 oz plain flour, sieved
1–2 tbsp caster sugar, for sprinkling

For the filling:
125 g/4 oz Quark
125 g/4 oz Greek yogurt
25 g/1 oz caster sugar
1 tbsp orange liqueur (optional)
grated zest of 1 orange
125 g/4 oz strawberries, hulled and
    cut into quarters

To decorate:
strawberries
icing sugar, sifted

Baked Stuffed Amaretti Peaches

1   Preheat the oven to 180°C/350°F/Gas Mark 4. Halve the peaches and remove the stones. Take a very thin slice from the bottom of each peach half so that it will sit flat on the baking sheet. Dip the peach halves in lemon juice and arrange on a baking sheet.

2   Crush the amaretti biscuits lightly and put into a large bowl. Add the almonds, pine nuts, sugar, lemon zest and butter. Work with the fingertips until the mixture resembles coarse breadcrumbs. Add the egg yolk and mix well until the mixture is just binding.

3   Divide the amaretti and nut mixture between the peach halves, pressing down lightly. Bake in the preheated oven for 15 minutes, or until the peaches are tender and the filling is golden. Remove from the oven and drizzle with the honey.

4   Place 2 peach halves on each serving plate and spoon over a little crème fraîche or Greek yogurt, then serve.

Ingredients   SERVES 4

4 ripe peaches
grated zest and juice of 1 lemon
75 g/3 oz amaretti biscuits
50 g/2 oz chopped blanched
   almonds, toasted
50 g/2 oz pine nuts, toasted
40 g/1½ oz light muscovado sugar
50 g/2 oz butter
1 medium egg yolk
2 tsp clear honey
crème fraîche or Greek yogurt,
   to serve

Tasty Tip

If fresh peaches are unavailable, use nectarines. Alternatively, use drained tinned peach halves that have been packed in juice, rather than syrup. You can vary the filling according to personal preference – try ground almonds, caster sugar, crumbled trifle sponge cakes and lemon zest, moistened with medium sherry.

Summer Pavlova

1   Preheat the oven to 150°C/300°F/Gas Mark 2. Line a baking
    sheet with a sheet of greaseproof paper or baking parchment.

2   Place the egg whites in a clean grease-free bowl and whisk
    until very stiff.

3   Whisk in half the sugar, vanilla extract, vinegar and cornflour;
    continue whisking until stiff.

4   Gradually whisk in the remaining sugar, a teaspoonful at a
    time, until very stiff and glossy.

5   Using a large spoon, arrange spoonfuls of the meringue in a
    circle on the greaseproof paper or baking parchment.

6   Bake in the preheated oven for 1 hour until crisp and dry.
    Turn the oven off and leave the meringue in the oven to
    cool completely.

7   Remove the meringue from the baking sheet and peel away the
    baking parchment. Mix together the yogurt and honey. Place the
    pavlova on a serving plate and spoon the yogurt into the centre.

8   Scatter over the strawberries, raspberries, blueberries and kiwis.
    Dust with the icing sugar and serve.

Ingredients   SERVES 6–8

4 medium egg whites
225 g/8 oz caster sugar
1 tsp vanilla extract
2 tsp white wine vinegar
1½ tsp cornflour
300 ml/½ pint Greek yogurt
2 tbsp honey
225 g/8 oz strawberries, hulled
125 g/4 oz raspberries
125 g/4 oz blueberries
4 kiwis, peeled and sliced
icing sugar, to decorate

Helpful Hint

Always remember to double check
that the bowl being used to whisk egg
whites is completely clean, as you will
find that any grease will prevent the
egg whites from rising into the stiff
consistency necessary for this recipe.

Index